"Ayesha's incredible courage and journey to step into opportunity and create new outcomes for herself, her family and her clients has been inspirational to observe. From the first time we met in Bangladesh, her home, I knew she was going to make things happen. From moving to Sydney with her son, starting a new career, being accredited in our brain-based NeuroTREAD programme and pursuing her interest in neuroscience, her book Mindspeed is a testament to her determination and passion to help people live their best lives."

Kristen Hansen
Author of Traction: The Neuroscience of Leadership and Performance.

As a NeuroTREAD™ Accredited Facilitator of EnHansen Performance, the key insights were mostly drawn from this book

Copyright ©2020 – Ayesha J Bibha
Published in Australia

All rights reserved. No portion of this book may be reproduced, stored in a retrieval system, or transmitted in any form or by any means – electronic, mechanical, photocopy, recording or scanning, or other – except for brief quotations in critical reviews or articles without prior written permission from the author or Samantha Jansen Publishing.

Author: Ayesha J Bibha
Title: MINDSPEED

Cover Design and Typeset by Ingrid Karm
Edited by Hayden Jones, 21C Editing
First Edition - Published in September 2020
ISBN: 978-1-63649-768-6
Subjects: Mindset, Personal Development, Self-leadership

www.samanthajansenpublishing.com

"Mindspeed is the state at which our mind operates effectively, by using optimal time and with the right amount of energy. In a world full of so much choice and confusion this book will help to create a powerful mind to drive us to our full potential."

Christina Guidotti,
CEO Leading Women, Australia

"For our HR LEADer Online Summit, I had a great chance to work with Ayesha who was very flexible with the organizational moments. Ayesha added value to HR professionals by disclosing the details of driving success as a leader backed up with neuroscience. Her expertise in the area shows professionals around the world the relationship between brain and leadership. Ayesha has also done extensive research in the area, but shares the knowledge in a compelling manner, which makes the presentation much more engaging and thought-provoking."

Mansura Mehdiyeva, Business Development Manager
ULead Media Group
Prague, The Capital, Czech Republic

"I recently attended a session on The Neuroscience of Leadership delivered by Ayesha in Auckland New Zealand. Her expertise on the matters of the brain as it relates to leadership is impressive and the research she shared is compelling. In today's global environment of leading a diversity of teams, Ayesha's wisdom is highly needed. She is able to take a complex topic – neuroscience - and not only make it understandable to non-scientists, but make it entertaining as well. Her presentation was filled with easy to apply actions. I look forward to seeing Ayesha in action again soon, and learning from her."

Lenora Billings-Harris CSP, CPAE, International Diversity and Inclusion Hall of Fame Speaker, Greensboro, North Carolina

"Ayesha is a trailblazer of the industry. I recently interviewed her for my podcast, Attitudeable, and her insights and different types of research opened a new scope of vision for the world. Your latest book is a revolutionary study of our minds. Thanks, Ayesha for helping all of us move forward and seize our lives and every moment of LIFE!!"

Dolores Guinazu, Language Consultant & Certified Translator, Buenos Aires, City of Buenos Aires, Argentina

"I have recently had the pleasure of working with Ayesha speaking through virtual webinars and planning future speaking events. Ayesha is a complete professional who takes great pride in her work which is only superseded by her passion for speaking and delivering her message. She is a very good speaker and has captivating presence both virtually and on the live stage. She is also very easy to work with. I would not hesitate in recommending Ayesha to any host organizers looking to fill their speaking event programmes."

Maxwell Muir, International Speaker, Edinburgh, United Kingdom

"I had the pleasure of hearing Ayesha speak at the Global Speakers Summit in Auckland. She has strong content in her field of leadership. I look forward to seeing her journey and thought leadership grow."

Jerome Joseph, CSP, Global Speaker, The CEO - The Brand Theatre, Singapore

"Ayesha J Bibha is a smart, brilliant and savvy Mentor with the heart and mind to help everyone win big. Ayesha rocks and LOVE HER WORK!"

Edward Zia, International Master Coach, Sydney, New South Wales, Australia

"Ayesha presented and spoke at the Global Speakers Summit in Auckland, New Zealand on her topic 'What's Hot's for 2025 - Neuroscience of Leadership'. Ayesha has great passion, depth & knowledge in her area of expertise. I was particularly intrigued with her model presented on the Brain Business and how she expanded on the Balance, Renew, Adapt, Integrate and Nurture elements as it related to leadership. Has been a real delight to see Ayesha in action and present on the insightful model of the Brain Business. Thanks and continue to inspire with your work Ayesha!"

Jonathan Low CSP, Global Speaker on Sales & Service Optimiser, Top 30 GlobalGuru, Kuala Lumpur, Kuala Lumpur, Malaysia

"Ayesha's breadth and depth of knowledge and experience in neuroscience, leadership and EQ are impressive. Her TEDx and Conference talks and Coaching programs are powerful, insightful and transformational. She is a world-class speaker, lecturer and coach. Her passion stems from three things: eliminating confusion and overthinking and replacing it with a solution-focused decision, removing exhaustion and defeat by restoring emotional control, and enabling style in work-life to live better."

Fleur Leong, Transformation & Change Culture Development Coach, Arete Quest, Sydney, New South Wales, Australia

"I attended Ayesha's presentation of 'The Neuroscience of Leadership' on GSS2018. The best part of her presentation is that she explained PFC, Limbic System and Amygdala in a very simple and easy to understand way. It made me more interested and want to discover more in neuroscience. Well done, Ayesha!"

Haiming Jiang, Motivational speaker, confidence coach and NLP trainer, A+ Coaching Ltd. New Zealand

MINDSPEED

HOW AMBITIOUS LEADERS CLEVERLY USE THEIR MINDS OVER TIME AND ENERGY

AYESHA J BIBHA

Contents

MINDSPEED

ABOUT THE AUTHOR

Ayesha J Bibha is a strategic thinker and is obsessed to ignite insightful thinking. In dealing with changes and adversity, she can foresee big impacts and plan the small moves toward solutions. In her speaking, writing, or advising, her number one intention is driving people's mind into the future, while many are stuck in the confusion of the past or present. In her works, her passion goes with three things: eliminating confusion and over-thinking and replacing them with solution-focused thinking; removing feelings of being overwhelmed and exhausted and replacing them with ownership; and provoking people to live better.

FOREWORD

Our mind is one of the most fascinating and most powerful things in the universe, and we all carry one around in our heads. That is literally mind blowing. The fact that we do not spend more time, energy and focus on developing this amazing tool of ours is - frankly - shocking. I can think of no other thing that would have a better return on investment in our lives than to fine-tune our own minds.

And that is where this book comes in. Because that is what "Mindspeed" does: it makes us think about the thing that makes us think.

No matter what your goals are in life, no matter what you find important or who you want to become: Your ability to better harness the unlimited potential of your own human mind will help you achieve what you want to achieve.

Fredrik Haren - The Creativity Explorer
Author of **The Idea Book** (included in the 100 best business books of all time)

ACKNOWLEDGEMENTS

I feel truly grateful to some people who have had a profound contribution behind making this possible. I want to thank them for their unconditional support throughout the time while I had to dedicate my time to staying focused on writing.

I have to start by thanking my handsome son, Ahnaf, who never complained about not getting enough attention while I was physically in front of him but mentally was creating the concept of the book. Moreover, I often heard him asking if I want to get some coffee. Love you mate, you keep me being ambitious to become a better person. I could think big for you.

I thank my parents for trusting me, supporting me, and always encouraging me to think independently what I like to do. Thank you, Fredrik Haren, for being my speaking mentor and giving me the inner theme of the book. I am grateful to Kristen Hansen, for mentoring me and introducing me to the world of neuroscience in leadership and performance. Christina Guidotti, who mentored me and became a role model of being a true believer, I am thankful to you for raising my belief inside of me. Thank you, Gretchen Managing Director Asia Pacific at Conversant, for having patience with me and guiding me through. I am also highly honoured for unconditional support from the tribe of Thought Leaders. Thank you Adam Voigt, Lisa O'Neill, Peter Cook, Richard Hodge, Paul Worth and many more. I am very humbled to Matt Church, who shaped me, challenged me, and made me a better version than I could hardly be. Thought leadership practice is a huge commitment and you brought my true self out to face it and accept it. Thank you, Matt, for giving new meaning to my being in the world.

Thank you to the beautiful soul, my Business Manager, Diana, you are cute and clever. You know me more than a close friend. Thank you to Samantha for helping me in finishing my book without trying hard to make it perfect. And many thanks to Hayden for giving insightful feedback for the book.

Thank you to my colleagues, clients, students, and well-wishers for your supportive gestures toward me and my works.

Thank you to those who stretched me big time in my 15 years of ambitious journeying, for you, I could become the person who I am today, I could keep the significant commitment to myself.

Thank you Almighty for granting me all resources that I would need in walking the path.

And finally, thank you, as you have chosen your time to invest in.

INTRODUCTION

I did not learn about Mindspeed
by practicing speed,
I learnt it from my shame
of having a slow mind.

Being an ambitious leader in this ever-changing work environment, you are working longer hours, giving more time and energy, while dealing with the high pressure of new challenges, automation, restructuring, or outsourcing. At the end of the year, at the end of the quarter or at the end of the day, once you sit quietly and evaluate your day, quarter or the year, you automatically evaluate it based on the time and energy you gave. In organisations, our KPIs are set where the baselines are time and energy focused.

In reality, you always wish to have more free time, more energy and to be more successful. But with a traditional mindset, free time and more energy does not come with success. To be successful you must take on high pressure - that's how your job is viewed as important to others, to your company or to society.

With the modern mindset of success, the economy is moving from outcome driven to people driven based on human capital. When success is measured by imagination and ideas, measuring success based on time and energy is not enough. We must focus on the mind to measure our performance. We need to be more inward focused, or more like 'inside out'. Measuring success based on time and energy is no longer a sustainable way. By managing the mind, we can create a positive ripple over our time and energy.

I want to give you a ground of awareness on how driving your mind will speed your success and help you to live better.

At the beginning of the second quarter of 2020, when COVID19 was isolating us from friend and family, when we all were pushing ourselves harder to accept the new normal of working online, the concept gave me a totally new dimension, a new meaning. The new reality made us realise that managing mind is not an option, it is a must. Our brain is not programmed to accept any difference; it will try its best to drive away from any change. But it is also true that staying away from change will never give us solution-driven directions.

In this book, it is my clear intention to bring an awareness of how you can manage your mind over your time and energy. You can be more effective in using these three key resources: *mind, time and energy*. I want to give you a ground of awareness on how driving your mind will speed your success and help you to live better.

This book is written with busy but ambitious leaders in mind who continuously strive for doing and being better, who are open to transition and change for better impacts and greater results.

Being an ambitious leader myself, we use so many tools and books to be better and more effective in work and life, but we still crave to be 'betterer' (a term often used by Matt Church). Having had the same intention over the past 5 years, it has been my conviction to work for a more meaningful life even while going through multiple transitions, both in my personal and professional life.

Central to this journey has been my professional attachment to the field of neuroscience and leadership, which has unveiled many hidden and unknown sides of being a leader. Working closely with around 350 ambitious leaders across industries in all 6 continents, it was a surprising journey of insights for me. At times, I shared these insights in the form of short articles, captured them in my personal journals and used them in my lectures, speaking, coaching and mentoring sessions. I became fascinated to see how they resonated with others. These insights were the shortest version of my deeper understanding of what ignited leaders in their work and life. It became my call to put them together in this book in a friendly structure that will help more leaders around the world.

While teaching a course to executive leadership students at the University of Denver, I was fascinated to develop the insights through conversations with them. The ideas are backed by the research-based findings that I have learnt, taught, advised, and practiced over the past 5 years. They made my existing perspectives stronger and gave new perspectives, new insights. They created completely new strategies through my experience of observing, sharing, facilitating, applying, and practicing the findings. My intention here is to give you some digestible bites of the findings that anyone can understand, practice, and get the benefit of.

Mindspeed is the state at which your mind operates most effectively, by using time optimally and with the right amount of energy.

Regardless of the role you are in, it is always about people and people are led by their mind. Throughout my work and life experience, I have felt it is my responsibility to bring out the meanings of more effective mind management strategies to help you in your professional and personal life. That is why I am introducing **Mindspeed** to you – it is the state at which your mind operates most effectively, by using time optimally and with the right amount of energy.

In a high paced environment, when change is obvious, staying the same is suicide. You need to be quick enough to cope with the pace of change, guided by an understanding that your time and energy are limited to support the work you need to do. This sounds hypothetically possible, but in reality, it is hard, hard, hard.

Added to these pressures, today we have social connections in the palm of our hand. We can easily become biased by others' opinions, diluted by seeing what other people are doing or distracted in our thinking which takes us away from our true priorities and focus. It takes courage to stay focused on your strategic move towards the change you want, especially when it is normal to be pulled back by old beliefs, proven practices, or accepted cultural patterns. Moreover, once you value the people around you and aim to make them happy above all else, you embed their expectations and try to make them feel good for the time being. Thus, we remain anyone but who we want to become and don't do what we really want to do.

> *Matt Church in his book called Next has said, "We have more choice than ever before, and yet we are more exhausted than we have ever been. We are more connected than ever before and yet feel more isolated, lonely, and discontent."*

It stands to the reason that you need to be in the pilot seat of your mind to overcome today's multiple challenges which can drag down the best of us. If you want to be more courageous with your thoughts, to be a more open and creative thinker then you need to be consciously aware of your own capability to think, do and feel. This awareness will enhance your control over your mind to function in an optimal state. And that is when your mind can lead the change toward what you want to become, to be the person worth becoming, the better version of yourself.

If you want your mind to work optimally, you need to be on the top of your mind in navigating, controlling and driving it to the destination you choose. And it is hard work. It is a constant process of making **decisions**, managing **emotions** and creating additional **habits**.

Writing this book is the best personal example I can give you of applying Mindspeed to decisions, emotions and habits. I was planning on writing the book for more than a year, but could not move ahead with it due to a series of personal and professional changes which sapped my mind so much that I could not focus. I had become a reactive device in every situation. Then I flipped it around to realize this was actually a great opportunity to just get down some genuine thoughts and insights toward the book! On the positive side I finished 2019 by sorting out exactly what I wanted to share through my book.

If you want your mind to work optimally, you need to be on the top of your mind in navigating, controlling and driving it to the destination you choose.

At the beginning of 2020, when I restarted the writing process, I gave 30 days to myself to finish the first draft before other commitments took over my time. It was important for me because I wanted to publish my book in one year of Thought Leadership practice. How could a book of 40,000 words be finished in 30 days? It was only possible by using Mindspeed. Because I had spent the past year analysing my own decisions, emotions, and habits, I could work on them simultaneously to keep me at my desk and finish the book.

For me, the most important habit for finishing the book was to keep writing - keep writing without fear of the limitations of my own writing skills, to keep writing without being concerned about the initial quality of every word or sentence. To keep on writing became my new habit.

The emotion that was involved in this writing process was a huge challenge for me. It was the emotion of forging my new identity, the identity for which I have worked in Australia for the past 5 years. This was my 10,000+ hours of blood, tears and sweat. This was the emotion of knowing that the book will bring joy to the people of my inner circle. It was also the emotion of being released from the scars that people inflicted along the path I have walked to find my new identity.

This all flowed from the decision I had taken to build the new habit no matter what to make the book possible – to be creative in finding a better way to do it, to remain focused on the topic, and stay on top of the flow with the right balance. It was like trying to remain standing on a skateboard or flying an aircraft through turbulence and taking control to reach the destination.

As you read on, you will see how decision is the launching pad for sticking to your one big task till you reach the end. You will understand how emotion is the fuel that you need to keep your balance throughout the journey. You too will gain an appreciation of how habit is the stage where you need to keep applying your mind to a task to get up your speed.

Decision is the launching pad for sticking to your one big task till you reach the end. You will understand how emotion is the fuel that you need to keep your balance throughout the journey

The topics covered by this book are broadly applicable, but the key focus remains the same - provoking aspiring leaders to be more effective in using their mind, time and energy while working in an ever-changing environment. The book is simply divided into three parts: decision, emotion and habit, with each part focusing on the three key resources: time, energy and mind. Each part contains ideas, insights, applications and conversation starters.

By reflecting on each of the chapters, you will be able to redesign your success map, which will keep creating new meanings over the time of your success journey. The new meanings will drive your solution-focused thinking by breaking comfortable and automated patterns and by exploring new ones that ultimately leverage a better living.

The book is a program that won't ask you to invest thousands, but you can use it to run as a self-directed program for yourself or you can run in-house for the people you work with.

You can use the book as an in-depth program for your self-development, or you can also have a buddy with whom you can be more accountable to apply the learnings and share the impacts.

Using the tools will make a difference not only in your personal life, but it will also create a wave at your workplace and will make a positive difference in the way you lead or manage others.

Use the insights of the book to get your mind set to go for a transitional journey. Apply the tools to carry out conversations that bring more meaning to your life as well as in your organisation, because change starts on an individual level. After all, you are the single most important ingredient in your business that makes the actual difference.

My commitment to you is that I will make these ideas reachable for you in a simple and friendly manner. Let's see how you can bring in Mindspeed from here.

Ayesha

THE WHY

"One's mind, once stretched by a new idea, never regains its original dimensions."
- Oliver Wendell Holmes Sr.

There is no other quote but this with which I could start writing about the why behind the idea. The most striking aspect of the quote is that it highlights how a great opportunity opens up for our mind whenever we face change or difficult situations. It's true our mind can be the place where we can get stuck for hours or years after an event of change. On the other hand, we can also drive our mind out of the change with better control and more freedom to travel in many different directions.

The era that we are in today is proudly called the VUCA world[1] , which stands for volatility, uncertainty, complexity and ambiguity. These are the real conditions and situations which keep interrupting our way of thinking; they also result in huge disruptions not only in the way we work but also in the way we live. We can face and solve many of these multifaceted difficult situations in a most simplified manner - by working on our mind.

The leadership ladder

The goal of this book is to help you stretch your mind to become an ambitious leader who climbs the ladder to step up to the next level of your leadership, whether at work or in life. Here we are not separating leadership levels into lower and upper levels. We are making a shift of our focus or attitude to create greater impact and higher results. We are not limited by level here; we are open and collective learners to take the best from the previous level to the next.

The leadership ladder below shows the journey we are taking through this book. The move of the leader is that they focus on what attitude they carry to climb the ladder to grow their leadership up. They are mindful of the impact of their leadership and its actions to create an extraordinary result. It is a journey of moving out from your comfort zone to reaching your milestone.

Team leaders make things better, motivational leaders walk the talk and success driven leaders are ambitious to reach new milestones. They multiply their own actions as well as the actions of others.

What type of leader are you today?

A functional leader, managerial leader, or a motivational leader?

How good are you with driving your ambition?

Undriven - *Dysfunctional*

Dysfunctional, focus on small me, culture of comfort, negative impact, null result

- At the undriven level, a leader feels lost, dysfunctional, and disappointed; they do not see possibilities, they don't want new changes, and they see change as a big threat to their survival.
- This level has a complete negative impact on life, at the workplace as well as with the people around us.
- They are reactive to their surroundings; they are deeply disappointed and take this disappointment as granted.
- They blame others or bad luck for negative situations.
- At this level they often become lazy and name it a culture of comfort.
- They start thinking small, hold self-doubt and get dependent on others to act on something.
- Their mind is in a busy loop of thinking the same thing again and again. They feel overwhelmed by thinking a lot, but don't find a way out and are unable to produce a result.
- They are confused about what they want and tend to continuously compare themselves to others or to past experiences.

- And they also put expectations onto other people but they do not ask or share, rather they expect to be understood, which creates a communication gap and ends with big conflicts.

Process Driven - *Functional*

Functional, focus on what, meet targets, 1:5 impact, equal results

- At this level leaders accept the process or system that is imposed and defined by the society or organisation.
- They are functional to do the work that is programmed by the family, society or organisation.
- They develop the specific skills to do it right and effectively.
- They are 'what' focused and feel happy by doing what is assigned to them.
- They are submissive to the organisational culture or social norms.
- They work hard and are able to meet targets. At this level they can produce a little impact and are able to meet expected results.
- At times they feel stuck or overwhelmed and look for the meaning of their life.

Levels	Mindset	Focus	Attitude	Impact
Mindspeed Driven	*Ambitious*	*Bigger me*	*Reach new milestones*	*Exponential*
People Driven	*Motivational*	*Why*	*Walk the talk*	*Collective*
Outcome Driven	*Managerial*	*How*	*Good to better*	*Linear*
Process Driven	*Functional*	*What*	*Meet the target*	*Equal*
Undriven	*Dysfunctional*	*Small me*	*Enjoy the comfort zone*	*Null or negative*

- When they see a person living a successful life and enjoying it, they also feel encouraged and hope to be like them.

Outcome Driven – *Manager*

Managerial, focus on how, good to better, 1:25 impact, sum results

- This is the level where leaders enjoy the appreciation of others and are happy to work harder to achieve better outcomes.
- They can manage others on reaching the expected outcomes by explaining or teaching them how.
- They can reach the target, are able to take small challenges to get the job done.
- They believe that hard work pays off.
- They are self-motivated by the future and make comparisons with past results to feel encouraged.
- They can work collectively to produce higher impacts and they measure success by summation value.
- They can make themselves miss out on the present and that leaves them feeling unfulfilled.
- In difficult times, when pushed to meet a deadline or make changes, their mind can become unstable and they struggle to manage the work and their team.

They easily get dependent on past experiences, so they seek approval. They have a tendency to prove themselves or avoid taking responsibility to play safe.

People Driven – *Motivational*

Motivational, focus on why, walk the talk, 1:150 impact, compound results

- This level sees the leader become smarter.
- Here leaders become more people oriented, engaged, influencing and motivating to achieve compound results.
- They are like a role model to others; they walk the talk.
- They are more successful in keeping the team at the same pace.
- They can encourage people to do better, to learn new skills and to be more supportive.
- Under people driven leadership, people enjoy working together, they feel connected and like they belong.
- People oriented leadership sometimes drives the culture of competitiveness, which may become a challenge to developing a collaborative culture among internal teams.

- This leadership can produce collective results but sometimes the scope is hindered by biased competitions.
- And they often measure success by recognition, designation and social status.

Mindspeed Driven – *Ambitious*

Ambitious, focus on bigger me, reach new milestones, 1:1500 impact, multiply results

- Ambitious leaders are the pro in keeping up with a success system.
- We stay continuously motivated with new success milestones.
- We consider a long-term game. We do not settle for short-term pleasures.
- This is the level where we are not over-confident, but we are often called ambitious.
- We hold a big vision and create ways to reach it.
- We have a clear idea on what we want.
- We have a deep level of self-esteem and self-trust. We own what we stand for and can take steps by securing non-negotiables.
- We have courage to challenge old beliefs, to reshape organisational cultures and to challenge social norms.

- We are open to trying new ways. We take failures as an advantage of trying different ways.
- In change or adversity, we do feel tired or overwhelmed, but also know how to treat those around us. We do not regret taking downtime or reflection time.
- We are deeply connected to our values and purpose.
- We have the courage to feel new emotions.
- We are aware to own control of our own mind when everything around us tries to drive it crazy.
- We focus on the bigger version of us, who can lead by example, lift others, create more leaders (not followers) and create a win-win culture.
- We are agile, resilient, and insightful.
- We can engage people, help them to improve their emotional awareness and challenge their old mindsets.
- We are purpose driven over profit oriented and take sustainable and lasting moves that produce results in cumulative ways.
- We can multiply results with exponential impact.
- We are the leaders who create leaders, shape the culture, and leave a legacy.
- We create ripples in the workplace environment that an organisation can find hard to measure.

In this book I am pointing to the people who are lead thinkers in their workplace, in their own business or in their own life. The key focus of the book is driving change to be the person that you want to become. It is backed by the neuroscience of leadership insights connected to social behaviours in the arena of self-leadership practices. In this ever-changing world, it is essential to stay stable, innovative and mindful with your own thoughts, time and energy. This book will challenge your leadership skills by adding more value to the way you think or act. You will become a more insightful, resilient, and agile leader.

Key Assumptions of Ambitious Leaders

"And those who were seen dancing were thought to be insane by those who could not hear the music."
- Friedrich Nietzsche

Ambitious leaders have an entrepreneurial mindset. They can think better in challenging situations. They are decisive, they have emotional awareness and they accept changes for better outcomes. They have a constant need to improve the skills they learn from mistakes and take continuous action on new ideas. In today's highly changing work environment, who would not like to work with a leader like them and even become one?

There are three key assumptions that leaders need to take on today to keep pace with change and their own ambitions.

1. Think beyond the possibilities

"When everything seems to be going against you, remember that the airplane takes off against the wind, not with it."
- Henry Ford, founder of Ford Motor Company.

Continuous progress is not a smooth road through creating new habits. It needs the readiness of making difficult decisions at the right times. It's the ability to control the emotions that come along with difficult decisions. In that way a leader creates a positive ground to push through the possibilities. When technological changes are obvious, restructuring is normal and disruptions are new disciplines for the business, a leader also needs to be at the same pace as the fastest changes, because being slower may cost a lot – both opportunity and money. When a leader's mind is ready to accept the challenge, they automatically program their mind to see the possibilities. They are far more comfortable with any discomfort as they have chosen the challenge, it is not given or imposed. This mental readiness gives the leader drive against all the odds to reach their goals regardless.

2. Innovation challenges the current practices

"Creativity is just connecting things. When you ask creative people how they did something, they feel a little guilty because they didn't really do it, they just saw something. It seemed obvious to them after a while. That's because they were able to connect experiences they've had and synthesize new things."
- Steve Jobs

The business environment today demands that leaders are innovative. Innovation starts from curiosity. When curiosity is converted into creativity, innovation occurs. In life, we also need to be innovative if we want to challenge the current practices and want to grow. Being innovative means being open to new ideas, new learnings, experimenting with new ways and adapting to the changes. By learning how to teach the mind to be innovative, it is like taking a road of positive changes. Once a leader knows how our mind works, they can lead an idea into innovation, interest into implementation, and curiosity into creativity. Innovation is the tool that jumps over time. Innovating new ideas can help a business or career to jump forward with additional prospects of growth and success.

3. Deep motivation drives extra miles

"The secret of change is to focus all your energy not on fighting the old but on building the new."
- Socrates

Leaders who are big picture oriented are not motivated by instant pleasures. They are not convinced of anything without consistency. They even would prefer to delay receiving gratitude to get long term recognition. They stay motivated for the long term to expand their success in multiple dimensions. They run a marathon rather than running a sprint. They do not hesitate to learn from failure, are not ashamed for seatbacks and are not afraid to change direction or reset it. But one thing for sure - they never give up. They know how and when to recharge themselves. They consciously choose the people to be around. They are upfront to say no to those who drain their energy. There is hardly any ambitious leader we can find who doesn't have an energy routine. They know how important it is for them to keep up with their physical, mental and spiritual well-being. That's how they manage their quality thinking and maintain a healthy mind.

An ambitious wolf will rise above a complacent lion.
- Matshona Dhliwayo

In a nutshell

Starting your own business, taking over a new role, or leading a new team are all exciting, rewarding and positive energetic things for an ambitious leader. Doing something new and bigger is always fearful to the mind; it takes more energy, effort and intense time. When the mind takes on new challenges, it starts comparing the present with the past self or others which often causes self-doubt and anxiety. These are all normal. This is how the body chemically gets ready to accept new challenges.

An ambitious leader must know the science behind the function of the mind. That way you will develop the capacity to help yourself and others, not simply managing your own mind. Owning control over your mind also creates a positive impact over the way you invest your time and energy. And the ultimate goal of the book is helping ambitious leaders like you to play a long-term game in a sustainable way by driving with Mindspeed. Let's explore more about the mind, time and energy.

[1]First used in 1987 in the leadership theories of Warren Bennis and Burt Nanus

MIND TIME ENERGY

Mind

"YOUR BRAIN WORKS BETTER WHEN YOU ARE INSPIRED TO BELIEVE, AND THIS MAKES EVERYTHING YOU WANT TO SEE HAPPEN ON AND AROUND YOU MORE LIKELY."
- MATT CHURCH

In English the word 'mind' can represent the brain itself, along with the essence of thinking, experience, behaviour, attitude and expression. The intention behind choosing this word is to make the topic easier to understand and bring relevance to your life. Focusing on the mind will generate more insights and allow you to implement your own strategies for your strategic moves in life or work.

Throughout this whole book, you will find me sharing some brain science around being conscious, creative and courageous. In my journey of life and learnings from my study, research, observations and through working with my speaking audience, coaching clients, mentoring participants and most importantly with myself, I found there are significant benefits of applying the knowledge of brain science. This experience has created in me a responsibility to share the insights that can help today's leaders to use their mind better.

Mind is a verb

In recent years, study of the mind has become the largest growing area of interest in leadership and performance circles. To create a basic understanding of brain science, let me give some ideas on this most complex and dynamic organ of the human body which produces our every thought, action, memory, feeling and experience of the world. It weighs in at around 1.4 kilograms, and contains one hundred billion neurons.

According to the evolutionary stages in the womb, our brain is a combination of three major parts, known as the reptilian brain, mammalian brain and human brain:

- *The* ***reptilian brain*** *is the oldest of the three. This part of the brain is responsible for our body's vital functions such as heart rate, breathing, body temperature and balance.*
- *It is also called the brainstem and the cerebellum.*
- *The reptilian brain is reliable but tends to be somewhat harsh, rigid, sensitive and compulsive.*
- *The* ***mammalian brain*** *is known as the limbic system.*

- *This part of our brain is responsible for our feelings and emotions.*
- *It can record memories of behaviours that produced agreeable and disagreeable experiences, or in other words our positive and negative experiences.*
- *The limbic system is the brain part which includes the hippocampus, the amygdala, and the hypothalamus.*
- *The mammalian or limbic brain is the place where we make conscious or unconscious judgments which has a strong influence on our behaviour.*
- *In short, this is where we make meanings which make us unique to others.*
- *The* **human brain** *is known as the neocortex.*
- *It is the newest area of the brain which is responsible for the development of human language, rational, analytical and abstract thought, imagination, and consciousness.*
- *The neocortex is a flexible zone and has almost infinite learning abilities.*
- *It processes all facts and figures but does not drive our behaviour, actions and attitude.*

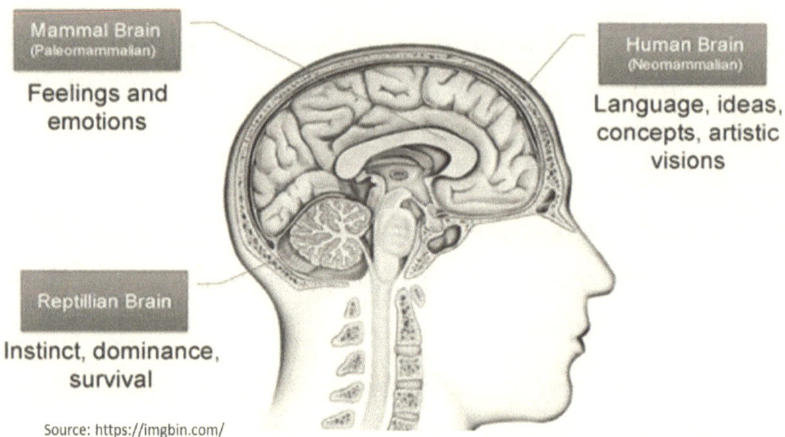

Source: https://imgbin.com/

These are the three broad divisions of our brain and they do not operate separately or independently. There are numerous interconnections among these three parts through which they influence and interconnect to one another.

Now, to give some ideas on the technology behind neuroscience and leadership, I would like to refer to fMRI (or Functional magnetic resonance imaging) scans which measure blood flow and the EGG or electroencephalograms, which measure the brain waves. Using them both, it is possible to measure in which situations our blood flows to which part of our brain and what the state of the wave is. If we can understand this, we can also understand what our choices could be to make our blood flow to make a particular part of our brain more effective. For example, for better decision making and logical thinking we need more blood flowing toward our thinking brain - the frontal lobe or specifically the prefrontal cortex.

In recent years, the study of the anatomy and physiology of the brain has given a new dimension to human thinking and behaviour. Technologies like fMRI, positron emission tomography (PET), and quantitative electroencephalography (QEEG) have amazingly helped researchers to find the link between our core physical organ (brain) with the pattern of our thinking, feeling, acting and perceiving. Based on the findings, the neuroscience of leadership professionals have made it clear that human thinking and behaviour don't work the way they were once perceived. This area of study has also discovered the inherent practice of brain biases, even in successful organizations.

This book will focus on only three key major parts of our mind and they are highly relevant to the executive functions of our brain including decision making, emotion control and creating new habits.

1. Prefrontal cortex (read more in Part 1)
2. Limbic System (read more in Part 2)
3. Amygdala (read more in Part 2)

The Prefrontal cortex is responsible for our executive function, and it's known as our thinking brain. The Limbic System is responsible for our emotions. And the Amygdala, located in the middle of the limbic system, is responsible for the 3Fs (Fight, Flight, Freeze) responses. Besides the key parts, you may also find some discussion on mind functions among those who are involved in driving change and creating memory.

Understanding the mind and the science behind it will help you to understand how to navigate and drive yours.

This book is more specific to creating awareness of your thinking, doing and feeling. As a result, you can be more creative, resilient, and agile in adversity, challenge and change. You will become more courageous in taking strategic moves for leading with lasting impact.

Mind = Think + Feel + Do

As a leader, we need to know how our mind works, by which I mean to understand the three basic functions of our mind:

1. Functions of our thinking mind
2. Function of our emotional mind
3. Functions of our learning mind

Understanding these three is vital as we make decisions, control our emotions, and create new learning connections to generate new experience as well as change. Without creating new experiences, we can never create a new milestone.

I have tried to shed some light on the broad understanding about our mind, its biological location and its anatomic structure with its basic functions. Next, at the beginning of the three parts to the book, I will take you a little closer to our mind and its functions to know how decision, emotion and habit works. I do not want you to understand everything at this point, but I want you to have a basic touch of neuroscience in leadership and performance. I would also suggest you come back here at the beginning of each of the three parts whenever you need during the book or once you have some insights in your work or life.

Now that you have some idea of our amazing mind, let's understand the other two key resources which are also hugely important for our performance, outcome, and success – time and energy.

Time

"Your time is limited, so don't waste it living someone else's life. Don't be trapped by dogma, which is living with the results of other people's thinking."
- Steve Jobs

We do many things a day, and different types of tasks require different types of work. Different types of work require different types of effort. But we often do not schedule our day based on the effort we need to pay. As a result, we take a longer time to finish and we end up being overwhelmed by work. Now the question arises, what time of the day are you most productive and efficient?

Key learnings on Making More Time

1. *Our mind cannot multitask.*
2. *In neuroscience, multitasking is switching - switching from one task to another.*
3. *Switching is the passing of information from the right to the left hemisphere through the corpus callosum, the part of the brain that separates two hemispheres.*
4. *Trying to do more than one task at a time decreases our IQ level.*

5. *Multitasking is only an external way of looking productive, because inside of our mind we cannot do more than one task at a time.*
6. *Taking a break every 90-minutes increases the mind's capability to be productive for the next 90 minutes.*
7. *Using time on multiple things is not only mentally ineffective but also takes lots of energy by increasing stress.*

Managing time is a fundamental need to be productive. In neuroscience there are some facts that will help with knowing about time management from a different perspective. It will help a high performing leader to be more successful in less time.

Select the information

A better decision is a result of selecting better information. We deal with information flowing from too many sources. With an overload of information, we get paralysed and we get confused. As a result, we can't move ahead, or we cannot decide. We get overly anxious about the situation and juggle the information. That takes our time as well as energy. When it is the time to make a decision, select the information and stick with that. Treat it creatively in the processing part but stay glued with the information you need and from whom you need.

This simple act creates some space and saves the energy of your brain to do quality processing of information.

Stop splitting

We have too many options to stay connected these days. We often split our attention by checking email, or other connected notifications. By taking away our attention, we stay on the surface of our thinking. We cannot reach insight, deep thinking or creative thinking.

When you feel the pressure of providing attention to too many things, you cannot distinguish between them based on urgency and importance. Pick one task at a time. Forget about others while working on one. Set a time to stay focused with the selected task. Prioritising your focus will help you to finish the task way faster and in a quality way.

Break to build

Our mind has a tendency of decreasing energy over the time of the day until we refuel it. Trying to stay awake or focused with caffeine does not work if you want to maintain a quality focus on your thoughts. It only keeps your mind awake.

Again, the mind has its most quality energy in the beginning of the day. Starting with the task which requires your best quality thinking is a clever way to save your day from being overloaded and working overtime. According to Gloria Mark, University of California, Irvine, who studied digital distraction, in every drop of focus you lose around 23 min to get back to the same level of focus after a distraction. Counting each 23 minutes is a lot at the end of the day or end of the week.

Take a systematic break throughout the day. Taking breaks will not separate you from the task. It will regenerate the energy that your mind needs to work better.

> *American physiologist and sleep researcher Nathaniel Kleitman has found that our mind can operate for 90-minutes with high intensity. And after 90 minutes our mind starts to produce stress chemicals which drain our energy.*

When you are stressed, you concurrently minimize the quality functions of your prefrontal cortex. You are not able to do much logical thinking and at that point you are more aroused by the emotional mind, and you often react with your behavioural dominance of flight, fight or freeze patterns.

Energy

*If you need to chase anything,
chase energy over the task.*

Like other parts of our body, our brain uses energy for mental functions. A typical person's brain uses approximately 10.8 calories every hour. And by the time you run out of energy, you also lose the capacity for quality functioning of your mind. You take a longer time to finish the work, you procrastinate, or you feel overwhelmed with little stress or pressure, so your body reacts, and you don't engage with the work.

Having an awareness of energy will allow you to plan your day differently. You will be able to remind yourself to chase the energy when you feel the need for it. You will prioritise the task to finish which requires quality energy. Otherwise, you will end up with a feeling of being overwhelmed, stressed, anxious, tired and eventually lost. Continuing with activities which drain energy will make you undriven. You will not be able to think, feel or do the quality thing that matters for your success.

According to a Harvard Business Review article, The Neuroscience of Trust by Paul J. Zak, compared with people at low-trust companies, people at high-trust companies report 74% less stress, 106% more energy at work, 50% higher productivity, 13% fewer sick days, 76% more engagement, 29% more satisfaction with their lives, and 40% less burnout.

No matter how resourceful you are or how often new opportunities knock on your door, if you don't find the right energy to grab the opportunity, you will never be able to progress. You will never be able to grow. You will feel lost and out of control of your situation.

You need to ensure that your energy is generated, managed and used toward the tasks that you choose. And for doing that you need to check that in three ways:

- The way we show our fortitude
- The way we flow out energy
- The way we fuel our energy

"My general attitude to life is to enjoy every minute of every day. I never do anything with a feeling of, 'Oh God, I've got to do this today."
- Richard Branson

Energy is not a tool; it is the lever

"Give me a place to stand,
and I shall move the Earth."
- Archimedes

A lever is used to move a heavy or firmly fixed load with one end when pressure is applied to the other. Levers can be used to exert a large force over a small distance at one end by exerting only a small force over a greater distance at the other (Wikipedia).

A lever is a great representation of our energy at work or in life. You can call it the pace or the drive. To be more effective, to be more engaged, or to create a better culture, energy is the tool that can multiply performance, thus driving our success milestones.

As an ambitious leader, it is your skill to manage scarce resources effectively. In most cases, we measure our success and performance based on the time and outcomes. You can measure the time or the outcome, but you cannot measure the energy. That's why we hardly think about our energy – our right mental state. However we now know that by shifting energy from negative to positive to leveraging, we can shift ourselves from reactive to responsive, and from a responsive to reflective work environment.

Responsive	*Positive*
Reflective	*Leveraged*
Reactive	*Negative*

In a high changing environment, which is already stressful and overwhelming, your job as a leader is to leverage your own energy first. By doing that you can create the ripple of energy around you at your workplace, with your team, at home, with your family members which will shape the organisational culture as well as the family norms.

If you feel lost, find yourself procrastinating, or not starting, you are not having a problem of prioritizing or time management.
You have a lack of energy.

Reactive

A place with negative energy is a place where people are not encouraged but rather blamed. It involves ball passing or passing off responsibilities; not having ownership and not asking for help or not supportive of each other. They are often in a competitive state and do not appreciate others. Here people are more reactive, they are easily annoyed and angry. They don't see any positiveness; they treat any change as a big threat. They have a lack of ability to manage their own energy or are unaware of being able to create positive energy.

Responsive

People with positive energy engage and motivate others. They delegate the task to achieve the outcomes. They follow the process to be more effective. They are responsible to meet their targets. They support others, appreciate others and give feedback for improvement. Working in a positive energy environment is engaging. People feel empowered and they follow leaders to drive toward a shared goal.

Reflective

With leveraged energy, people enter the learning zone. People are inspired by others. They take ownership and have the courage to think differently or creatively. They are proactive in offering support; they ask for feedback and work with others collaboratively like a family. With leveraged energy people feel rewarded, secure. They have core confidence and self-trust. This gives them the certainty which activates the open learning centre of their mind. They become highly adaptive to change.

With energy, you can make a big difference. Regardless of how big your ambition is, chase energy and your success will chase you.

"ENTREPRENEURSHIP IS A GREAT LEVELLER, THE WONDERFUL THING IS THAT MONEY IS NOT THE SOLE CURRENCY WHEN IT COMES TO STARTING A BUSINESS; DRIVE, DETERMINATION, PASSION AND HARD WORK ARE ALL FREE AND MORE VALUABLE THAN A POT OF CASH."
- RICHARD BRANSON

ERA OF MIND

If you do not own your mind and take control during change, change will take over your mind. In an ever-changing world, if you decide to bring about change in yourself, then the place where you need to start is in your mind.

Here's 10 reasons why the mind matters more than ever in life and work today.

1. Leadership is impact driven and impact creates memory

The key difference between impact and outcome is one is long term and the other is short term. It is essential to be long term impact focused if you want to make a sustainable result in your life. This comes with anything that you do, from buying a pair of shoes to investing in a house. It becomes easier to decide if you just ask once whether it is an impact driven act or an outcome driven act. That's how you also can easily separate yourself from being influenced to take any decision which may not serve your future. By doing this, you also have a better balance between your rational mind and emotional mind. By touching on the feelings or emotion associated with the thought, we can create an impact that lasts longer in our mind, because impact creates memory. The greater the impact, the stronger the memory.

2. Mental effectiveness is the productivity prerequisite

According to Nasa Scientist, Dr Rita King, "The imagination age is the theoretical period beyond the information age where creativity and imagination will become the primary creators of economic value. This contrasts with the information age where analysis and thinking were the main activities."

We cannot stay dependent on analysing and thinking now that the world is seeking more innovation in every small thing that we are doing. Thinking and analysing are sometimes very liner ways to solve a problem and at some stage we can rely on systems for that. On the other hand, having an out of the box idea, we need to harness our mental efficiency, by which I mean, enabling full brain thinking. Linked to this, your decision or action also demands you to be more dynamic to enhance the real productivity of yourself.

3. We all are unique with different approach of thinking

Throughout the generations of lived experience, each one of us is unique with our unique way of thinking. This is at the same time an advantage as well as a disadvantage for us. It is an advantage for us once we view it as diversity and it is a disadvantage once we consider times when we need to align our thinking with a shared goal. And the connecting point is when we need to know what is the right thinking which will take us toward what we aim to achieve, and for this it is necessary to know how our mind works.

4. Mental capital is the fuel of shared value

In the way that we invest in an asset to get value over time, we also need to treat our mental capacity as capital that we can invest in to gain something worthy. It is not about being strategic or productive only, it also means we need to monitor more closely our mental fuel for generating greater value.

5. Today's work and life demands quality way of thinking

There is a slight difference between "quality thinking" and a "quality way of thinking". The quality way of thinking means not being distracted, being more mindful, having less biases, not being influenced or manipulated. Only a great level of awareness can stop us from having a non-quality way of thinking. Being more aware about the function of our mind can also help us to know how to generate the meaning of our thoughts.

6. Mind is the vehicle of growth today

Once we consider our life as a journey or evolution, we can view it as a path that we walk over our lifetime. We can finish it by taking the known or expected path or by taking the unknown-adventurous route. It depends on how ready our vehicle is to drive through the journey. This is where our mind takes the place of a vehicle that we drive. No matter whether you are a good driver or not, the fitness of this vehicle matters the most to take you on the adventure of doing something bigger and out of the box.

7. We are time travellers, not moment creators

The increasing dependency on a digital lifestyle has produced in us a shorter and shorter attention span. We enjoy scrolling down and checking the news quickly; we enjoy having the remote control in our hand and constantly changing the channels to check what is better. Similarly, we also want to make changes to life issues quick, being quicker in whatever we are doing, even making a million dollars quick! Our customers want quick services, our boss wants quick actions, we want quick solutions.

Sometimes we also travel to past experiences and future expectations to generate a solution. By doing this, we are constantly pulling our future into the present or travelling between past and future. By doing this, we are missing our present reality, we are not fully aware of our present opportunities to create more moments, and this is essential if we want to be more creative over being analytical. Moreover, being quick is a threat creator when we get better results slowly. The pressure of acting quickly easily makes us overwhelmed and stressed. And a stressed mind cannot be creative.

According to a Google study, 90% of people who own multiple devices switch between an average of three devices per day to complete a task.

8. Change is normal, and disruption is expected

Being the citizens of the VUCA world (Volatility, Uncertainty, Complexity, and Ambiguity) , we must agree that change is the new normal, and being resistant to change is not. If you are stopping yourself from being adaptive to change, you are not normal. There is no way you can afford to waste your time by resisting change. It is the time to be clever in handling the change.

A Harvard Business Review survey in 2016 found that the most important skill in transformation is the ability to adapt.

Creating an adaptive mind is the first place where we need to start working on facilitating any change. No matter if it is big or small, a change is always a source of fear for our mind. And understanding the right way to treat the change is the key.

9. Quality connection comes with boundaries

In a society of connection, we cannot ignore staying connected. We cannot avoid being reached anytime. We cannot have control over our inbox to stop receiving emails that are not on our agenda. But we can choose our responses. This is where the quality comes. Knowing how, when and where we need to create boundaries makes a big difference in our decisions or actions.

10. Managing mind is the strategic initiative

It is no longer the time to manage time. Now is the time to be better in managing the mind. Mind is the single most important unit that comes above anything that we do. Managing time is a functional competency, whereas managing mind is a strategic competency that anyone can develop to lead success out of themselves or out of their team. It is the era of developing the skill of being clever in using the mind to perform the right functions – creative, analytical, effective or routine. If we take our life as a long-term project, it is crucial to master the skill of managing mind and bringing harmony among the rational, emotional, creative or intuitive functions or our mind.

"When the mind is compassionate, it is calm and we're able to use our sense of reason practically, realistically, and with determination."
-Dalai Lama

To keep up with the pace of change in the economy, your organisation, your productivity or lifestyle, our ways of dealing with time, energy and mind also need to be changed. And once you are ambitious, you enter the game with acceptance and readiness to learn.

In the next few pages, let's explore the mind, time and energy more closely.

MINDSPEED

By using the mind, we can create new habits which allow us to use our time better by making the decisions that matters and by bringing the right emotion to generate the right energy to drive toward our success milestone.

How do some people become hugely successful with the same amount of time as the rest of us?

How do some people make a huge success out of their extreme failure?

How do some people rise above the line?
What makes them cutting edge?

These questions persisted in my mind over the past 5 years of study and over a decade of experience in working with people from all over the world. They turned me back to myself and gave rise to a formula that changed everything that I think, feel and do.

This formula that I used with people with whom I worked is:

Mindspeed = Mind X (Time + Energy)

In the formula:

- *Time and energy are two factors that we use to do anything, and mind is the multiplier.*
- *Time is the constant and we all have the same amount of time.*
- *Energy is the variable which depends on the situation and the emotion that we carry.*

- *Mind is the coefficient that multiplies the outcome positively or negatively.*
- *Any negative value of time or energy will impact the outcome or impact that we create.*
- *In a nutshell, it can produce an exponential impact on our outcomes if we focus on mind first.*

The multiplier that can leverage your time as well as energy is your mind. Knowing the science behind it gives you the guidelines that work. If you decide, feel and take small steps that matter, time management and energy allocation will follow.

It is possible when we wear the lens of our mind to see our time and energy quite differently. By wearing the lens, we can clearly see the 3 key functions of our mind: decision making, emotions and habits.

To sharpen the vision forward, you need to change how the mind learns to think better, feel better and act better.

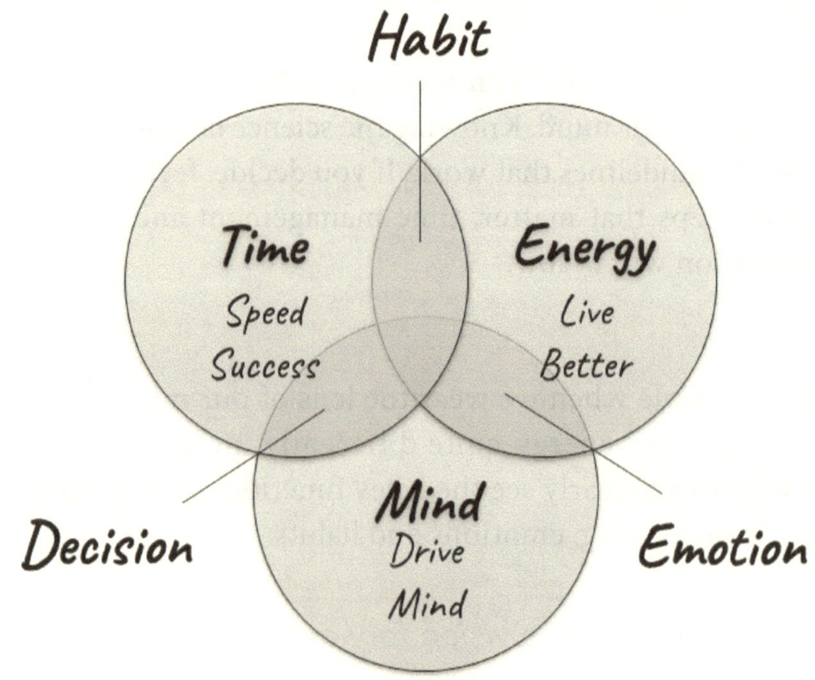
Habit
Time
Speed
Success
Energy
Live
Better
Mind
Drive
Mind
Decision
Emotion

There are many books written on success systems among which the most popular ones are based on building habits. Authors have even proved that a good habit can make incremental success over the year. But my observation, application, research and findings say that a success system starts from a decision, whereas habit comes after.

You need to work deeply with your decision, not quickly.

You need to accept, own and feel the decision.

You need to be the decision.

Decision increases the focus; it keeps you building the right habit. If a habit makes the outcome 1% better every day (James Clear 2018), then a habit founded on the right decision multiplies the 1% every additional day. And emotion is like the fuel, you need to filter the fuel based on the decision as well. When you know what fuel causes you to flow - how you are best encouraged, inspired and stable with your decision - you move in the right direction faster. That is when you grow exponentially.

When you decide to pursue your ambition, you are often seen as selfish (or a bit insane!). With ambition some people walk far away from their core self and some people rediscover themselves. Personally, I am a fan of being ambitious. Being ambitious is about continuous growth, continuous personal development and readiness to embrace the change over time. It is not a mission or project with a beginning and an end. It is a process or system to create new success milestones over time.

You might be a knowledge worker working for a company or a leader running your own business; being ambitious means you have a strong desire for continuous success with lasting positive impact. And our workplaces as well as society need more ambitious leaders.

9 steps of being a Mindspeed leader

Mindspeed is your optimal mental state where you can travel through your courageous, conscious and creative mind to plan, manage, create and act on your leadership strategy.

1. Courageous decisions

Courageous decision making is a mental state. To achieve this with your Mindspeed, you need to start with your courageous decision making potential - the courage of making a decision for the bigger cause, the courage of staying with it till the end, the courage of seeing, feeling and thinking of the change. This is the stage when you are able to say to yourself: 'I accept it and I use decision making as my power to do something bigger than me'.

Once you accept it, you also own it, which can totally change the game of dealing with your time and energy.

2. Clear intention

Your intention of reaching the destination will let you find a way to reach there regardless. You are not going there when everything is supportive or available. You can find the way anyhow. You know where to say no, what not to listen to, what not to follow, because you are clear about the yes.

3. Firm fortitude

To sustain the game of creating continuously successful milestones, you need to build the emotional muscles to be able to deal with it. Once the environment is highly changeable and you are facing adversity, being resilient is the key and developing fortitude is the way.

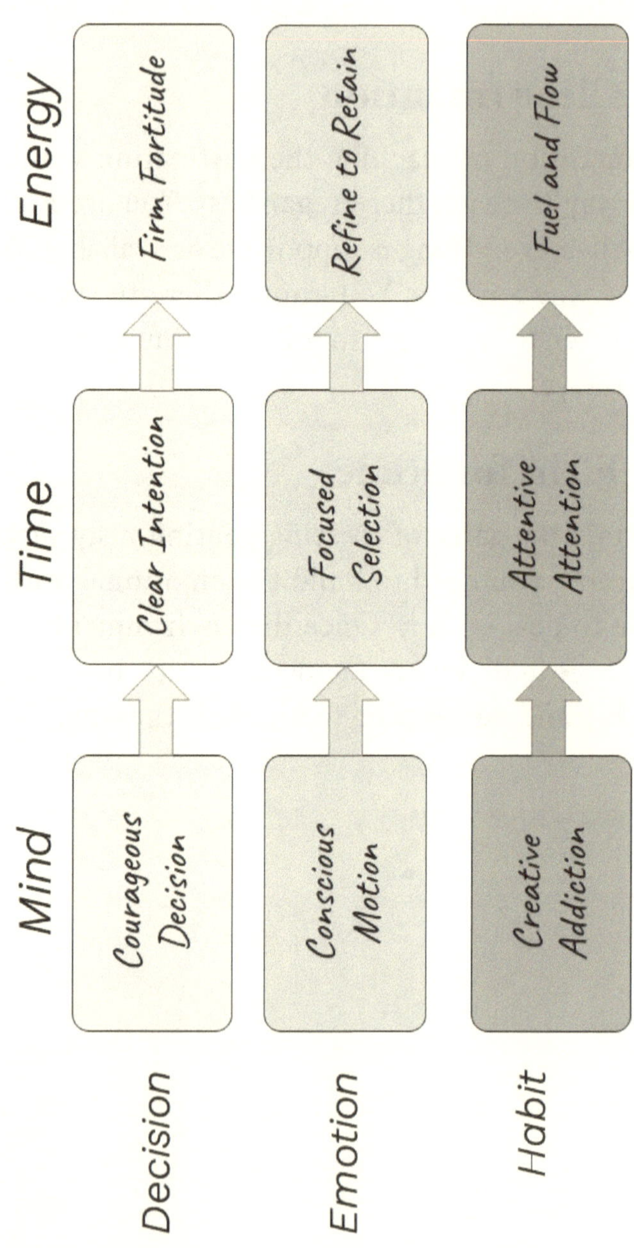
Mind
Time
Energy
Decision
Courageous Decision
Clear Intention
Firm Fortitude
Emotion
Conscious Motion
Focused Selection
Refine to Retain
Habit
Creative Addiction
Attentive Attention
Fuel and Flow

4. Conscious motion

Being conscious of what you think, act and lead will create a conscious motion. It is a deep level of work within your emotions. You need to rediscover your own core emotions, your deep level emotional memories, and your connection to your feelings. By doing this you will be transparent, authentic and reflective of your true self. Your conscious motion moves you from inside out.

5. Focused selection

Imagine you are in the driving seat and you need to park your car at the curb side to take a parcel out of the back door. Sitting in the right driving seat, you aim to park on your left and not scratch or hit the car. To make this simple manoeuvre, where do you need to pay attention? Is it the curb or the car? Only by paying attention to the curb, can you reach the curb. Likewise, in your life, once you are in the driving seat and trying to drive, paying attention to what you do not want or do not want to become is the wrong focus. It leads you to waste years trying hard, but not trying clever.

6. Refine to retain

The source of fuel matters for the quality of living. Trying to be super economic when choosing fuel can cause long-term damage to the engine. Working in a toxic place with toxic people can cause long-term damage to your health, both mental and physical.

7. Creative addiction

When you are facing adversity on your journey, when you are unsure about your every turn, you need to be addicted to being creative. You need to be always curious and ready to accept new changes that spark creativity. If you are dealing with a team, you need to encourage them to remain creative by allowing them to think differently.

8. Attentive attention

Attention is a unit of action that you take repetitively to lead to a desired outcome. With a continuous and repetitive rotation of wheels, towards one direction you drive your vehicle forward to reach a destination; similarly, achieving a successful milestone is a multi-year journey. It's a journey where you will experience the turns, ups, downs, and ditches, but you must keep moving. You will find some people joining or leaving you, but you must keep your attention right without being distracted by external influences. This is the game of being consistent and gaining incremental reach through attentive attention.

9. Fuel and flow

When you drive a long route, it is routine to fuel your vehicle to keep it moving. Likewise, you need to take rest to recharge your mind, to keep up its flow and function better. As a human you need to consider your wellbeing; rest and slow down time to be sustainable with your Mindspeed.

Now ask these questions to let your mind start working in the background while you proceed to reading the next parts:

- What are the unconscious thoughts occupying your mind most?
- What are the unproductive tasks you invest your time in now?
- What is the most unimportant issue to burn your energy now?
- What percentage of your day is passed on unimportant, unproductive and unconscious tasks?

DECISION EMOTION HABIT

If you are sitting in the cockpit of your aircraft to reach your success milestone, your decision mind helps you set the destination and the direction to fly to it. Your emotional mind acts like the control stick and your habit works like the autopilot mode.

We make decisions based on logic, calculation, comparison, analysis, data, facts, findings and figures. We make better decisions by processing our experience, trends, insights and assumptions. It requires the complex processing of information to make the decision better.

In decision making, we are not always logical. We are strongly influenced by our emotions and memories which create the meaning of the decision that we are taking and they encourage us towards that. So, a better decision must be made with a better understanding of your emotions. But even if we decide, we are often distracted when our emotions get stronger than our decision. We often recall old emotional memories and it becomes our habit to revisit decisions over and over again. Have a look at where emotion sits in this table:

Application	*Tools*	*Impacts*
Decision	Mindset and Reward state	Acceptance, ownership, purposeful, innovative
Emotion	Self and others emotional control	Mental strength, readiness and wellbeing
Habit	Consistent in incremental habits	Strategic steps, aligned, adaptive

To break with the continuous pattern of our mind, we need to take a decision that aligns with the new emotion that we want to feel. That's how we can create new mental wiring for new habits. Emotion is the glue between your decision and habit.

We often read books on habits and try to start creating a new habit based on understanding all the good reasons for creating that habit. But it does not work if you do not fully understand the decision. It's like wanting to be a good public speaker and you start creating a habit of reading lots of articles on your topic and then building a habit of writing articles on the topic but never putting it into practice; it will never make you a great public speaker.

Before you create a new habit, no matter how tiny that is, you need to be clear on your decision. You need to know how this small habit will serve you in your success milestone. You need to be clear how badly you want to reach that and how important it is to create the habit, because creating a new habit is easier than breaking an old one. It takes time and effort. Give your time and effort based on a long term and sustainable reason.

Making a decision based on the facts and logic without emotion is not sustainable. Having an emotion without decision does not change the situation. A habit never sticks without being backed by decision and emotion.

How do you make decisions, how do you handle emotions and how do you form new habits?

PART 1
DECISION

Set directions to the destination

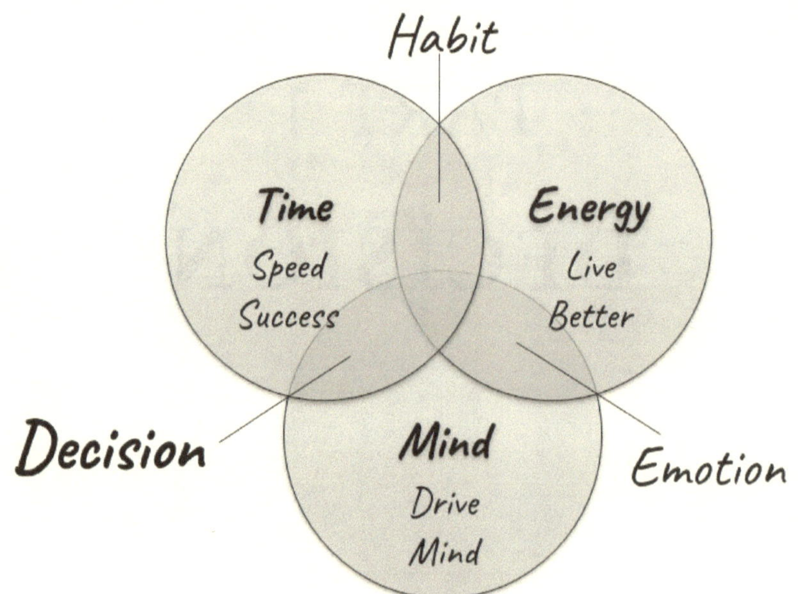
Habit
Time
Speed
Success
Energy
Live
Better
Decision
Mind
Drive
Mind
Emotion

Mind, Science and Decision

The yes-no state

Our mind is always conscious about our safety and survival. This is the reason why it constantly scans the environment to find if there is a threat or a reward for us. By threat we mean anything that may cause a problem to my survival, it does not matter if it's a small or large threat. Reward means opportunity, good words or gratitude. According to Dr. Evian Gordon MD, PhD, Founder and Chief Medical Officer of MyBrainSolutions, safety is the brain's core organizing principle. Most other functions are subservient to this need.

Key Learnings: Threat-Reward

1. *Our mind is always generating information by* ***scanning the environment****. According to science, it scans the environment 5 times per second. By scanning, our mind identifies whether the environment contains a threat or a reward for us.*

2. *If we are in a* ***threatened state*** *our outer vision narrows, we try to avoid risk, we have less insights, and we are less connected. Moreover, we are problem focused, not solution driven.*

3. *If we are in a* ***reward state****, we become broad focused, we are open to risk, we can have more insights, we are more connected, and more solutions focused.*
4. *Threat or reward is also* ***non-conscious****, we don't even have to be consciously aware that we are in a reward or threat state. Positive or negative clues in the environment can put us into a threat or reward state.*
5. *We have the* ***power or ability*** *to put ourselves into a reward or a threat state by creating the environment which is positive or negative for them. And we can do that even by faking that we are in a reward state, because our mind cannot distinguish between real and unreal, it simply scans and makes a judgement.*

I remember once I checked my email and found an invitation for a new project. Reading this email made me feel instantly good. I sat and started looking for information that I could put into making the profile relevant to the project. It took a few minutes but left me feeling good for the whole day. The reason behind this good feeling was nothing but being conscious of what I had done, not what I needed to do, or what I could not do. Even such a small thing can create a reward state in our mind, so I started feeling more confident, more valued. I felt confident by reviewing my good work and

I felt more valued because they asked for my profile for a bigger project. My insight is that once we can consciously drive our feeling forward, then we can also bring real motion to anything through the right emotion. Then we can choose to pay attention to the things that matter and create progress.

The biological area of our brain known as the Prefrontal cortex is the part of our brain which is responsible for all our conscious thinking. That's the reason why it is also called the executive brain. By using this area our mind makes decisions, solves problems, does logical thinking, understands information, recalls information from long-term memory to help analytical thinking and create greater meaning.

In short, our mind decides, recalls, plans, understands but also inhibits by using the Prefrontal Cortex. Here inhibition means stopping our mind from thinking a certain way because it is not supporting us in feeling good. And this is very important for me, because I believe in everything we do, we do to feel better, to feel happy. The following are the key learnings about our conscious mind that helped me in my time of adversity. It is my intention to make them as simple as possible to allow you to quickly apply them to your life as well.

Key Learnings on the Prefrontal Cortex (PFC) – The Decision Mind

1. *Our PFC is* **always busy** *and active whenever we are awake. It keeps our mind busy by nonstop thinking, analysing, comparing and inhibiting.*
2. *Physically this is only 4% of our brain but it works all the time and uses lots of our mind's* **energy**. *It is worth adding here, working all the time does not mean it is working on quality thinking.*
3. *By mind-energy we mean availability of* **two ingredients** *- the glucose that we intake every day with our food as well as with our breath. The energy flows into our mind through blood flow which contains these two ingredients of mind-energy, oxygen and glucose.*
4. *The* **quality function** *of our conscious mind depends on the quality of the energy flow it has. By this I mean if you have not eaten much food, if you have not taken enough glucose and/or are not getting enough oxygen, your conscious mind cannot perform to its best potential.*
5. *Over the day, we gradually lose the capacity of our mind to work in an optimal state. Our conscious mind can perform better as long as it has enough glucose and oxygen (mind-energy). According to neuroscientists, on average we can work for* **4 hours a day** *with our mind at optimal thinking,*

analysing, decision-making and inhibiting capacity.

6. *The more we* ***inhibit*** *ourselves from doing something, the more mind energy we use.*

1. MIND: COURAGEOUS DECISIONS

Courage is a decision with the right mindset to meet a long-term goal.

A courageous decision is a decision that you will stick to no matter what. It is a decision which impacts your life for the long term. It is a decision for which your next generation will be thankful to you. Deciding is easy but staying with the decision over the changes is the toughest job. A courageous decision is the key measure of success for ambitious leaders. As an ambitious leader, you know why, and you have the right mindset to carry the decision forward.

Making the right decision

"Whether you think you can or you think you can't, you're usually right."
- Henry Ford

As a Mindspeed driven leader you must have the readiness to make the right move with courage. This readiness means you can identify the move that you want to take. You want to see the change; you want to take up the necessary challenge and want to get ready with the instruments to drive the change. Being ambitious and success driven means you can:

- Find your decision
- Set a long-term goal

The very first step of your courageous move is deciding the decision. It is not simply about making the decision, it is about choosing what decision you want to make. It is about being fully clear about what big change you want to make, what big move you select to lead.

Deciding the decision is not easy. It requires both your physical and mental readiness. You must be able to choose one and leave others behind. You must give priority to do something over others. You cannot stay generous to everything that you like to do. You must be brave enough to say no often. In the book called *The*

Thought Leaders Practice, by Matt Church, Peter Cook and Scott Stein, it explains that the word 'decide' comes from the same family of words as homicide, suicide, regicide, and genocide. The suffix '-cide' has the root meaning 'to kill'. 'Decide' literally means to kill off the alternatives.

Imagine if you decide to go for a drive north. You must stay with the route that takes you north. You can plan to explore sites on the way heading north, but you cannot plan to visit some sites in the far east or west. It will not only delay your time, but also will drain your energy, and increase your fuel cost. If you want to enjoy a long drive you can take that route, but if you want to enjoy the most direct one, you must kill the alternatives first. Killing the alternatives keeps you stable with your decision.

Deciding is being generous, kind and fair to yourself

Clear is Kind, Unclear is Unkind,
Confusion is Cruel

You can only identify and clear up other thoughts by deciding on something. To me, most of us suffer with the moments before a decision is decided. Being indecisive is the toughest time and at the same time torturing. It is the time when you are afraid to be uncomfortable and accept the unconscious confusion.

In the book called *Dare to Lead*, Brene Brown wrote:

> *Over our years of researching and working together, we've learned something about clarity that has changed everything from the way we talk to each other to the way we negotiate with external partners. It's simple but transformative: Clear is Kind, Unclear is Unkind. I first heard this saying two decades ago in a 12-step meeting, but I was on slogan overload at that time and didn't even think about it again until I saw the data about how most of us avoid clarity because we tell ourselves that we're being kind, when what we're actually doing is being unkind and unfair.*

Now ask yourself these decision reflection questions:

Are you leading the move? ____________________________

Do you see the worth of the change? ____________________

Are you ready to accept the discomfort? _______________

Can you take the cost of not leading the move?

____

Do you have the persistence and passion that is required to get there? ____

How would you feel if you make the change?

____

Resistance to change is not a decision

"You can never cross the ocean unless you have the courage to lose sight of the shore."
- Christopher Columbus

Resistance to change is an emotion over decision. The feeling question is very important to answer here. Your commitment to answer this question is crucial. Take your time to search for the right emotion word or words and write them in the box below. Because most of us can identify the need for change, we do calculations, analysis, and get information to focus on external factors that can be achieved and changed. The missing information that we often don't give much importance to is our feelings and emotions that come with the change process.

Clinical Professor of Psychiatry at Harvard Medical School, Srinivasan S. Pillay, in his book *Your Brain and Business – The Neuroscience of Great Leaders* wrote:

> *When there is resistance to change, it is very rarely a missing thought process. Most often, it is a missing emotion. Coaches or managers can say to leaders 'When you are trying to make a change, your brain has to assess the pros and cons of your decision. Before you act, the accountant (PFC) in your brain does a quick calculation, but it relies on more than just your rational thinking to do this. It also relies on your emotions. How would you feel*

if you were to make the change?' This will allow leaders to add the emotional component to their analysis more readily and that will move them closer to change.

Moving closer to change is not just rational thinking, it is also a feeling. You cannot bring the readiness in you by simply calculating information, value of the cost, gain or threat and reward of your move. You also need to blend the emotional values of the risk and return.

Threat	*Reward*	*Move*
Informational worth		
Emotional worth		

Take your time to list the informational worth, threat and reward. Most commonly we measure them based on financial terms or external assets. Consider your emotional worth as well. Consider your feelings, using Robert Plutchik's 'Wheel of Emotions' (see at the end of the book) to list your emotions in relation to the decision. Consider the worth of your relationship to others who are also a part of the move process. Consider the worth of lifestyle change and personal development. On top of it, always keep the long-term worth in mind over the short-term excitement. This leads to our next understanding on the evaluation tool for taking a tough move or a hard decision.

When you are committed, you don't do it when it is convenient, you do it regardless!

Tough decision equation

Now the question comes, how do you know which decision to take and which to leave? What are the factors you need to consider?

In answering these questions, I would refer to the equation introduced by the New York Times best-selling author and high-performance coach and the author of *High Performance Habits,* Brendon Burchard. Here I would also like to add ROR (return on relationship) to his equation. To me, people with whom you are surrounded matters the most to keep up your right mindset, your energy and your Mindspeed.

$$\textit{Time} + \textit{Energy} + \textit{Resource} + \textit{Money} + \textit{Sanity} < \textit{ROI} + \textit{ROR} + \textit{FV} + \textit{PD} + \textit{L}$$

The meanings are defined below:

T = Time

E = Energy (physical and emotional)

R = Resources

M = Money

S = Sanity (mental and emotional)

ROI = Return on Investment

ROR = Return on Relationship (*people who support your journey, which is hugely important for your success fuel)*

FV = Future Value

L = Lifestyle (improved, healthy, wellbeing)

PD = Personal Development (that which serves who you want to become)

These factors are a good start to choosing the opportunity, to take the risk and most importantly to take the decision. I came across this equation in 2015 and I took my decision to move to Australia by leaving a respectful mid-level job with security. At that time, I could see the bigger picture by putting my decision into the equation. I realised the factors on the left side (TERMS) would be a huge investment for me. But I could also see the greater return on future values, lifestyle changes and personal development. This equation teaches you to think strategically by making a decision not only based on the short-term ROI, because that is a balance sheet mindset. You need to make a decision that serves the future as well.

On the other hand, if any factor in the left side (TERMS) gets higher, that directly impacts the factors on the right side. Like, when you try to stay highly focused on one job, you tend to pass the whole day and long nights by staying focused on that one thing. But staying too focused takes a lot of mental energy which has a direct negative impact on your lifestyle as well as your performance.

This equation is good to work through and connecting it back to planning every week is helpful. It allows you to have an insight into the total balance of your work and life, as well as outcome and efforts.

$$\mathit{Time} + \mathit{Energy} + \mathit{Resource} + \mathit{Money} + \mathit{Sanity} < \mathit{ROI} + \mathit{ROR} + \mathit{FV} + \mathit{PD} + \mathit{L}$$

By observing the factors, it is helpful to understand where I am increasing the cost or under-considering the value. What are the factors I need to minimise to make others better? Say for example, if you want to improve personal development, you also need to allocate some time by not compromising your key necessity time, i.e. sleep time.

State your current situation for each factor:

Time = ______________________________

Energy = ______________________________

Resource = ______________________________

Money = ______________________________

Sanity = ______________________________

ROI = ______________________________

ROR = ______________________________

FV = ______________________________

PD = ______________________________

L = ______________________________

Courage is setting a long-term goal

The term 'whole mind' means holding your whole mind present while thinking about the next move. Your logical thinking with emotional inclusion can open the pathway of intuition, although it is not easy to drive on all these roads. It is a practice; it is a balance and moreover it is a harmony.

The whole mind meaning is the most important thing before moving forward. This can bring a great level of self-confidence to take the leap. It helps you avoid that feeling of regret after. It allows you to uncover a new belief in yourself, having a deeper level of trust of your strengths. This is where stability is established because being the leader of new change, you need to remember change does not change, stability does.

- **Logical mind:** be conscious about your values, beliefs and purpose
- **Emotional mind:** turn all your emotions and trauma into passion
- **Creative & Intuitive mind:** taking new ways and following them without being influenced

Mind based goal setting

Being courageous is much more internal work than external. It is less visible and more invisible. Even if you say yes to change, walking through the process of change is hard work. I do not mean physically hard work only; it is a thousand-times harder mentally since you need to keep yourself motivated in the middle of a deep sea full of uncertainty.

How do you stay stable and consistent with the goal?

How do you bring the right attitude to handle the process of change?

How do you stay motivated once the road is uncertain?

A long journey with a little navigation can make a difference. Likewise, a change is difficult without a reward system. After you have made a choice and taken a decision, the reward system works like an extra accelerator. An increased commitment comes after making the decision. You need to use this information as a pathway to lead through difficult decisions.

The next activity is unfolding the decision into a small moving action toward your big move. This will also be a goal setting action plan framework. In any personal leadership development book, it is very common to talk about goal setting for a self-directed change. It will not be very different here, but the approach is differently integrated. Here I am bringing together the fixed-growth mindset theory, right-left mind function and habit-reward activation framework to make change easier and self-motivated.

In 1981, George T. Doran introduced the simplified version of setting a goal for the leaders across the globe. His concept of SMART goals represents five key factors to set a goal: Specific, Measurable, Achievable, Relevant, and Time-bound. This highly popular but decade old goal setting process is not enough when you consider the human factors behind the goal. This is because as humans, our mind is not purely a logical thinker, it also feels emotions.

This is covered by the SAFE goal setting approach. SAFE is the qualitative measure to our goal setting, which focuses on our creative and visual way of setting the goal. SAFE stands for See it, Accept it, Feel it, and Express it. Again, Dr Carol Dweck, author of the book, *'Mindset: The New Psychology of Success'* introduced a different dimension of our conscious or subconscious beliefs to pursue change. To make any change move, you have to have the right mindset. You have to believe that change is possible (*Dr Rock, 2010*). Having a growth mindset helps people to challenge the current culture or norm. If you consider the difference of perspective of the growth and fixed mindsets, the picture may look like this:

Open to move	*Closed to move*
I am ready once I decide	I am not ready yet
Every new part is required	A part is not working
Do it once and stay with that	Trying many ways for same reason
New move makes it more integrated	New move will make it complex
More thinking is creating a stronger connection	More thinking is creating more confusion

The whole-mind goal setting framework will help you to develop SMART and SAFE goals to unfold the fixed and growth mindset. From there you can then draw the action attention map for working with your growth mindset factors and moving out from fixed mindset factors.

All you must do, keep your decision as a stable ground and then bring other factors that support it.

The leading leadership consultant, Kristen Hansen in her book *TRACTION – The Neuroscience of Leadership and Performance*, wrote,

> *".. in any changes you want to make, don't expect your existing wiring to go away, it will not go away. Whatever it is that you have as a habit will stay there, but it will get less and less attention if you put more attention to something else. And attention is a positive thing that changes the brain."*

She continues:

> *"that essentially just means be more mindful of what you are wanting to change and pay attention to by having a Goal."*

The wanting and staying with that is the key. What you rightly want, want it deeply, then the mind will then start working along that pathway. It will start creating the route map to find a way forward. You must believe that, own that and need to be open to walk the journey through. That's when you will be able to have a fixed mind with your goal, but have a growth mindset to achieve it, to be the person you want to become.

- You see the pathways of driving towards the solution
- You are open and flexible but determined to reach the end
- You are stressed and tired at times, but you are not reactive and avoiding
- You experience negative emotions but also know how to turn them into passion
- You are interrupted and distracted to stay focused, but you can see the end result and you are certain of that
- You know the people from whom are you are receiving energy and the people from whom you are learning

Your next courageous decision...

Mindset you have vs Mindset you need

Fixed	*Growth*	*Fixed*	*Growth*

Define the courageous decision

Left Brain	*Right Brain*
S =	*S =*
M =	*A =*
A =	*F =*
R =	*E =*
T =	

Decision equation

TERMS < ROI + ROR + FV + PD + L

Decision

" ____ "

How does this framework work?

- keeps your big courageous decision as the base
- considers the decision equation factors
- covers both short term as well as long term elements
- works for both right brain and left brain personalities
- the goal is attacked through analytical and creative minds
- easy to identify the fixed mindset where it needs some work to enhance a growth mindset

The most important part of the framework is it will help you to become passionately rational about your move. It will give you the route map before you start driving. Ask yourself:

- Why are you moving?
- How long will it take?
- Who is involved?
- How will people support you?
- How does it fit your current network?

Being excited is comfortable.
Starting execution is courageous.

2. TIME: CLEAR INTENTION

"When your goals are clear, you will come up with exactly the right answer at exactly the right time."
- Brian Tracy

Your intention of reaching the destination will let you find a way to reach there regardless. You are not going there when everything is supportive or available. You can find the way out anyhow. You know where to say no, what not to listen to, what not to follow, because you are clear about the yes.

Know the no, find the yes

Setting a priority is like setting the attention compass and navigating your attention in the direction you are heading.

If you do not know your no, you will always be asking yourself whether you are on the right track or not. You will be confused on what you are doing, which will lead you to a feeling of being unsure and unfulfilled. There may be good milestones of success on your pathway, but you will remain indecisive, unclear and incoherent. The worst experience you can have is for your mind to be fuzzy.

On the other hand, setting a priority is certainty, being clear about not only (on) what you want but also what you do not want. And that is the time when your mind can easily distinguish between what serves and does not serve you.

Setting priorities gives you the clarity in your mind to be so clear that you do not need to go back to your previous state of thinking – the loop of overthinking. You can pay attention to what matters with confidence, you are not influenced or manipulated to do short term visible works to get a hit of dopamine in your mind. You are rather calm, light and peaceful with deep thinking to multiply the value of your work. And most importantly you know when to tap into your creative, imaginative, productive or autopilot mind.

Priority means saying no to say yes. Considering the yes makes a bigger impact over saying no.

Shallow work to deep work

Once you are setting the priority, it is important to stay with that only. Staying with that does not mean only doing that leaving others. It means putting all your quality mental energy into one big goal that matters. Let me illustrate this with a story about a middle-aged woman in a senior management role.

Samiha started 15 minutes earlier today. She had a very important meeting and didn't want to join the meeting without thinking through her preparation. She can still remember the embarrassing pause after asking for clarification in the last meeting with the group HODs.

She is feeling good about arriving earlier today. So she thought she'd have a coffee to cheer her up for the meeting. There she met Shelly and had a conversation with her about her recent project. Then she quickly visited her desk and noticed her smart-phone blinking a notification for the meeting. While checking it she also became curious about seeing what people were talking about her new dress that she wore to last night's party.

About a dozen comments and half a century likes, which made her feel quite good and by that time the 3 minute prior notification was blinking. Now she has just realised she is not prepared for the meeting.

It is easy to be attracted by all kinds of small things when you are not sure about your big thing

The bottom line is not being obsessed with social media or being noticed. This story is an example of what we often do when we are not aware of our deep attention and deep thinking. It becomes easier to be distracted by all kinds of small things when we are not sure about our big things, like checking email, having unnecessary long conversations with peers etc.

Distraction is the absence of deep work (Cal Newport, 2012). In the book called *Deep Work*, Newport also wrote,

> *"Professional activities performed in a state of distraction-free concentration that push your cognitive capabilities to their limit. These efforts create new value, improve your skill, and are hard to replicate."*

Being a knowledge worker of a company or an entrepreneur in today's business world, we all are struggling to use most of our mind power while working with a continuously engaging and interruptive environment, due to increasingly pinging devices or attention stealing open-plan work spaces.

Setting your time away from common and expected connection activities comes with huge courage. Once you know you are a part of the imagination era, where you are capitalising on your mental capacity to create economic value as well as a quality lifestyle, it is the right time to take that courageous leap.

> *Deep works are the professional activities performed in a state of distraction-free concentration that push your cognitive capabilities to their limit. These efforts create new value, improve your skill, and are hard to replicate*

Disruption-free deep work is also strongly suggested because securing your mind and energy from distraction is also known as "avoiding multitasking" in the study of science-based leadership practices.

Our mind is not able to do quality work while multitasking.

> *MIT neuroscientist Earl Miller notes that "our brains are not wired to multitask well...when people think they're multitasking, they're actually just switching from one task to another very*

rapidly. And every time they do, there's a cognitive cost." Another study at the University of London showed that subjects who multitasked while performing cognitive tasks experienced significant IQ drops. In fact, the IQ drops were like what you see in individuals who skip a night of sleep or who smoke marijuana.

Some studies have shown that even the opportunity to multitask, such as knowledge of an unread email in your inbox, can reduce your effective IQ by 10 points! The constant thrill of a new bolded email in our inbox keeps us ever distracted.

Multitasking is nothing but an illusion of looking busy, because it can only drain your cognitive capacity and drag you away from the deep work state.

So, multitasking does not work. You need to get rid of it to make better use of your cognitive capacity into something that matters most. Multitasking is nothing but an illusion of looking busy, because it can only drain your cognitive capacity and drag you away from the deep work state. Once you can avoid multitasking you can do deep work – direction free traveling of your mind from short term to long term memory, rational to creative thinking.

The deep work state is the distraction-free attention time. This is the time we can travel at high speed with the lowest amount of energy burning. It covers the mileage as well as the efficiency of fuel.

Similarly, once you know how to reach your deep work state, you can access your memory of prior experience and your present knowledge to process and to make a decision.

The deep work state is the distraction free attention time. This is the time we can travel high speed with low energy

Deep work is complex processing using the skill of blending present understanding as well as past memories and experiences. This is the next level of cognitive competency that you can achieve for multiplying results but in a flexible way.

- Deep work does not mean you always need to be 100% distraction free, rather you choose when you are allowing the distractions.
- It is not about being too much strict with time or too fixed to the goal, rather keeping some quality free spaces or downtimes in between.
- It is not about removing everything or everyone which doesn't serve the goal, rather making a priority of where you pay your attention. It is not

about being separated and isolated to be creative, it is about being with everything and having filtered thinking that makes you able to see your ideas happening around you.

Letting go of good, getting the great

Prioritising means you need to let go of other things and this letting go is to let yourself attain something bigger. This is where you have to be courageous and let go to stop spoiling your mental energy. By doing that you will free some space to allow new things to form – a new habit, a new lifestyle, a new skill or a new direction of thinking.

In short, you have to make your YES bigger than your NO. Whatever you say NO to have to have lesser value than what you choose to do as your YES. Here I mean the value is the sum of your return on investment, return on relationship, future value, lifestyle, and personal development.

Whatever you say no to have to have lesser values than what you choose to do as your yes

I remember when I left my country, I had to let go of many things. I had to let go of my job, I had to let go of a better job offer, known people and the environment. I had to let go of family and friends, my neighbours and colleagues. I had let go of the feeling that I will not be able to see my parents for many days. I had to let go of my mid-level career image and social status. I had to let go of the comfort of having a driver waiting and breakfast ready on my table before I left home for work. I also had to let go of the beautiful clothes and all my plans with my closest friends in my home country.

Letting go of my emotions and feelings was really hard, very hard.

Even if you let go, the emotion remains inside of you, and they keep looking for a small chance to come out and take control of your thoughts, and behaviours. And if you are working on something alone, it's normal that you will get hijacked emotionally very often. In your tired moments your emotions will take over all your attention or priorities.

It is like, converting current into electricity and converting emotion into passion.

To take control over these excessive emotions (panic), developing a self-directed thought that allows you to see the bigger value more often helps a lot. It keeps you in the optimistic mindset and if you master it, you can use this strong emotion to convert that into a strong passion. It is like converting current into electricity. Convert emotion into passion.

- How do you manage the emotion in those times?
- How do you comfort yourself to let go at that very moment?
- How do you be comfortable in letting go of the good for getting the great?

"Saying no to the wrong things creates space to say yes to the right things."
- Mack Story

Here's a personal example I'd like to share with you:

So, I sat down with myself and asked if I had any options left at that moment of deep discouragement. I had no option except to return to my country. But that also was not an option that I wanted to follow because I am not a person to lose the battle. So, I said to myself I had to make something more than what I had to let go, something in my lifetime that would never let me feel regret. Something that would be highly worthy to invest my time, energy, resources and most importantly my sanity in. Something that may cost all of my emotion in letting go, my existence and my comfort but would give me more than all that once I am done with my time here.

And I investigated my deepest self - what do I want to get out of myself? And the one condition was to do it without the investment of money. All I could invest in was me and my time, because I had no money to invest except buying my necessities. So I invested all my skill and time to create great value out of myself, that I will always be proud of.

Turn your discomfort into emotional courage. Make uncomfortable become comfortable. This means doing something very different. The acceptance will not be easy once everything is different around you and you are trying to do something different. There you will experience a strong fear of belongingness. It will keep pushing your attention and passion away. Take this as normal and start accepting that this is because you have reached the point called breakthrough. This is the point from where you are moving from being your good to becoming your great.

Breakthrough is the point from where you are moving from being your good to being your great

Stay light and playful

Listening to advice from Matt Church, the author of the book called *Amplifiers*, he talks about the power of motivational leadership to inspire and influence, which gives us a relaxed feeling. This ability to relax is important once you are working on your mental drive and cognitive productivity.

You cannot keep your attention stable if you are stressed. You cannot pay quality attention if you do not enjoy what you are doing. If you are playing a bigger game, you have no option but to calm your mind first. I'm not talking about a situational occasion like doing a meditation class or going for a relaxing day out once in a month. It is vital to stay calm all day at all times. Stay calm, light, relaxed and playful even when you are working deeply on a critical thing.

You cannot pay quality attention if you do not enjoy

Good to great is a long-term game. You cannot compromise with energy or sanity to achieve a long-term gain. That may bring higher returns, but it does not bring higher future value in life. Bill Gates says, "Most people overestimate what they can do in one year and underestimate what they can do in ten years."

- Stop overestimating what you need to do now
- Stop overestimating the value that it is bringing now
- Stop overestimating the waiting time to see the result now

Keep doing the work, stay light and playful, raise higher slowly. Be courageous enough to accept the slow lasting process to achieve great change.

Rat-marathon or rat-race

If you are caught up with the competitive struggle for wealth or power, you cannot play the long-term game. A long-term game has a direct connection with having more stable growth than the fluctuating spike. It is not about the amount your efforts are producing now, but it is about the continuous growth of the result.

Being competitive is good. It is hard to survive without having a sense of competitiveness in the real world. A competitive mindset works very well when you are highly focused on achieving a goal for a specific time; a goal that better serves you and the people around you for the long-term; a goal that gives you more than what you have invested to achieve. It is about investment, investing time, energy, resources, money, and sanity. You are paying attention to spending these into something by taking a portion away that you used to do before. You are taking away the portion from others who are also a part of your life.

You can only pay more attention to one by taking attention off from others.

- How do you keep the value of relationships when you pay less attention to your time, energy, resources, money, and sanity going into their lives?

- How do you keep the communication transparent with others?
- How often do you bring some certainty in the conversation with them?
- Do you take some time off to play the long-term harmony game?

If you don't, you will turn the rat racing mindset into a rat marathon mindset. You will always evaluate your move based on the outcome only, not on the quality of lifestyle or personal development it is bringing in you as well as to the people around you. And it is not a sustainable option.

But yes, a marathon is a long-term game with patience and stamina which might at times be demotivating as you don't see the instant outcomes. You need to remember the end repetitively and you need to learn to celebrate small successes.

"Pixar has been a marathon, not a sprint. There are times when you run a marathon and you wonder, why am I doing this? But you take a drink of water, and around the next bend, you get your wind back, remember the finish line, and keep going."
- Steve Jobs

The 5X5X5 game

If what you are working on is not going to matter in 5 years, don't spend more than 5 minutes being upset by it or by investing in it. Count to 5 to get back to your original focus. Once you are playing a strategic game, set yourself for a long term move to remain fixated on your priority. This rule will help you in ways like:

- Being in a positive mental state
- Having a forgiving mindset
- Seeing the new opportunity out of every 'no'
- Being stress free and unattached to what did not work

This will give you the advantage to grow, adapt and learn from challenges. You will be less likely to wait for the perfect moment because you know you are the creator as well as the controller of the perfect moments. Once you can create that for you, you also can create perfect quality moments for others who matter to your life.

If it is not going to matter in 5 years, don't spend more than 5 minutes on it. Count to 5 and get back to your original focus.

3. ENERGY: FIRM FORTITUDE

FORTITUDE IS THE MARSHAL OF THOUGHT,
THE ARMOUR OF THE WILL, AND THE FORT OF REASON.
- FRANCIS BACON

To sustain the game of creating continuously successful milestones, you need to build the emotional muscles to be able to deal with it. Once the environment is highly changeable and you are facing adversity, being resilient is the key and developing fortitude is the way.

"FORTITUDE IS THE GUARD AND SUPPORT OF THE OTHER VIRTUES."
- JOHN LOCKE

Fortitude, or resilience in today's language, means knowing how to cope in spite of setbacks, or barriers, or limited resources. Resilience is a measure of how much you want something and how much you are willing, and able, to overcome obstacles to get it. It has to do with your emotional strength.

People who are more resilient are capable of adapting to adversity. Resilient people can manage the stress caused by life changes, whether they are large or less significant. (Exploring Your Mind 2016)

According to Princeton's WordNet, the word 'fortitude' means "the strength of mind that enables one to endure adversity with courage". It is about adversity and courage. While looking up the relevant word, it is interesting to find words like patience, still courage, endurance, calmness, passive courage.

It is not about being quick to take decisions, or having a sense of urgency to take the decision now.

It is about being light and playful (as mentioned above thanks to Matt Church).

It is about building mental muscles slowly.

Like with dieting, you can find ways to reduce your body weight faster, but it is not always a healthy way to stay in shape.

Fortitude is about staying with the game with pace and grace.

The fuel and the flow of your energy develop your fortitude.

Emotional current into energy

Your courageous decision of doing something different and to shift the paradigm also comes with an emotional risk. To sustain the long-term game, you also need to build mental muscles. You need to be able to deal with emotional turbulence to convert strong negative emotions into a productive passion.

You are not playing a short-term game here, it is a long-term game; you are not running a sprint, it is a marathon. Surviving is much more important than showing off.

Building mental toughness may sound a hard thing to do, but actually it is about taking small actions towards building the right muscles. This is where Matt Church, the founder of Thought Leader Business School says, "be light and playful".

It is a serious game that you are playing in a playful manner. We often do not think like this, but the moment we think it is light and playful, we also encourage our reward centre to be activated and to be creative in doing the hard jobs. It is more about loving than healing.

Courage comes with emotional risks.
And emotional risks take lots of energy.

Sit back silently and see

One very common expectation that we carry about being successful and creating success milestones is that we need to make success visible.

You need to remember; success may not be visible all the time.

Be comfortable with that.

It is highly important to remind yourself about calmness. To be silent when you could talk, to be observant when you could take action, to do nothing when you could push toward something. This stillness is important for building mental strength.

It is the maturity of being able to deal with the present while aiming at higher success.

Un-comfortable

If you decide to develop fortitude to take your next step, the first thing that you need to decide is your next discomfort.

In what way do you want to be uncomfortable?

Be comfortable with the discomfort.
That is your stretching target to break old records of endurance.

Lead with positive motion

"STRONG FOCUS ON MATERIAL DEVELOPMENT AND ACCUMULATING WEALTH HAS LED US TO NEGLECT OUR BASIC HUMAN NEED FOR KINDNESS AND CARE."
- DALAI LAMA

Doing something different and unusual comes with the need to develop mental muscles.

When you work from a place of revenge, anger, aggression and competition, you burn more energy than the energy you need to do the work.

A leader in the world of change needs to be mindful, selfless, and compassionate. A strong focus on making money or creating wealth may lead us to be selective as a result and become unkind to people around us.

"A smooth sea never made a skilful mariner, neither do uninterrupted prosperity and success qualify for usefulness and happiness. The storms of adversity, like those of the ocean, rouse the faculties, and excite the invention, prudence, skill and fortitude or the voyager. The martyrs of ancient times, in bracing their minds to outward calamities, acquired a loftiness of purpose and a moral heroism worth a lifetime of softness and security."
- Author Unknown

Optionless

Once you know the meaning,
no rule, restriction, or reason can stop you.

Reach the island and burn the boat.

I love the term 'burn the boat'. Seth Godin often uses it in his blogs. It resonates for me so much because it made me think that I had only one way in front of me – to finish what I started in this book.

If you want to drive your success milestones, you must stick to the decision. You cannot think about plan B. You only can be the person you want to become, be the identity you want to carry, be the leader of your dream.

You cannot be tempted to do something easier and to stay comfortable. You must go through it. A long-term game must come with lots of challenges and it has ways to teach you how to become the new you.

It becomes less time consuming when you tell yourself that there is no boat. That's the place where the magic starts. You start going through. Because it is now what you have chosen with no way back.

SUMMARY: Part 1 - *Decision*

The most important part that every leader does in an everyday situation is decision Making - in decision making, we are actually choosing one thing out of many. The study of decision making has a goal that you understand the fundamental requirement of a process of choosing from multiple alternatives and coming up with one optimal action that you will be taking. Self-awareness and self-control have to come together to make sure a leader can make a better decision. Our self-awareness and self-control can help to generate positive social connections to encourage the collaboration, engagement, and influence among the people with whom we are working.

Courageous decisions - it's a mental state where it can be a total game changer for dealing with your time and energy. Being indecisive is a torturing moment but the key to remember is that deciding is being generous, kind and fair to yourself. In making a decision expect that there will be some resistance to change and it is an emotion over decision we often don't give much importance to - our feelings and emotions that come with the change process.

Clear Intention - Learning to say no to things and understanding the consequence of saying Yes.It's not going to be easy but you will find your way anyhow. You have a clear understanding of your yes, therefore you know what to say no to, what not to listen to and what not to follow.

Setting a priority teaches you this, meaning you are putting all your quality mental energy into one big goal that matters. Remember that you have to make your YES bigger than your NO. Whatever you say NO to has to have lesser values than what you choose to do as your YES.

Firm Fortitude - The fuel and the flow of your energy develops your fortitude. In an environment that's highly changing being resilient is the key, developing fortitude is the way. ***"Reach the island and burn the boat."*** You cannot be tempted to do something easier and to stay comfortable. You must go through it. A long-term game must come with lots of challenges and it has ways to teach you how to become the new you.

PART 2
EMOTION

Navigate and control the route

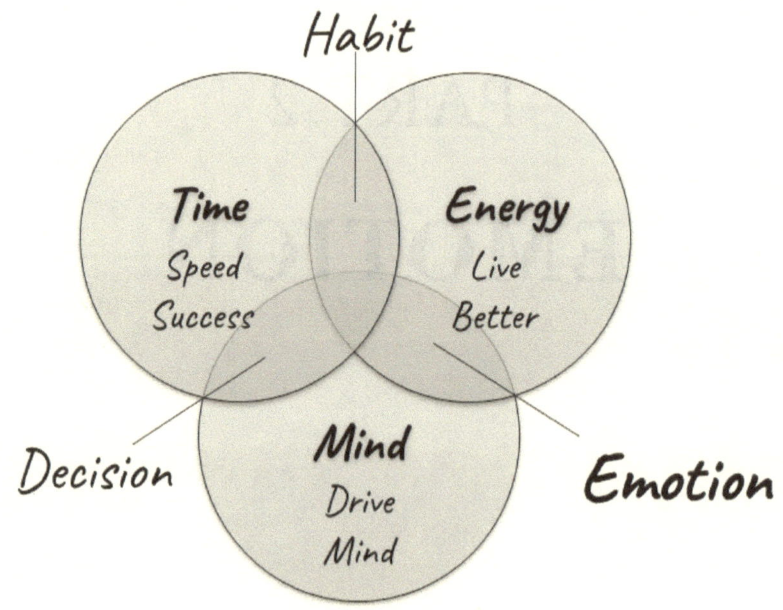
Habit
Time
Speed
Success
Energy
Live
Better
Mind
Drive
Mind
Decision
Emotion

Mind, Science and Emotion

That's why, this is how

Key Learnings on the Limbic System – The Emotion Mind

1. *The middle part of our mind is called the Limbic System, that deals with three key functions:* **emotions, memories and arousal**. *In humans, it is more involved in motivation and emotional behaviours.*
2. *Within the Limbic System, there is one key structure known as the Amygdala. Amygdala is also called* **survival mind**, *because it is involved in detecting fear and preparing for emergency events.*
3. *Functionally, the amygdala is responsible for the 3Fs Fight, Flight, Freeze.*
4. *It is also responsible for both creating* **awareness** *of emotions such as anger, fear, and sadness as well as* **controlling** *them. It also stores the memories of emotional events to be able to* **recognise** *similar events in the future.*
5. *In stress, under pressure or in a difficult situation, the blood drains away from the Prefrontal cortex and flows to the heart-lungs-limbs, to activate*

our Fight-Flight-Freeze response, and motor functions.

6. *When we are in the Fight-Flight-Freeze situation we can't think straight, we cannot think logical or rational, we tend to be reactive to the situation depending on the past experiences of our life.*
7. *If we train ourselves, we can have a more calm and rational response to threat situations.*

4. MIND: CONSCIOUS MOTION

Don't be yourself, be a conscious self, who thinks, acts and behaves (tuning) to the music you have deep inside.

Being conscious of what you think, act and lead will create a conscious motion. It is a deep level of work within your emotions. You need to rediscover your own core emotions, your deep level emotional memories, and your connection to your feelings. By doing this you will be transparent, authentic and reflective of your true self. Your conscious motion moves you from inside out.

Being conscious is a deep connection

There is a clear reason behind writing this part of the book. I want to share my learnings over a time of turbulence that will help you grow through your difficulties. This may sound a selfish goal and I do not hesitate to agree, yes, it is. In fact, I have heard this word 'selfish' many times. It's what has made me rather more determined to use the word and I am doing it very consciously. Today I have a completely positive and powerful meaning of this word that I truly own.

This ownership came through a consistent exploring of the meaning and through an endless effort of asking questions of myself over more than 10 years. Becoming conscious is a journey and it takes time. Even if you compare your consciousness before and after reading this book, it will be different. It is my promise to make the difference happen for you. So, you may ask, if this is a journey, what made me choose this topic to start with? Here is my honest answer: I want you to be ready with your full attention to be a conscious you.

Once you have a blending between your past, present and future, you are at the optimal state of using your conscious mind.

The journey of consciousness gave me not only the answer to my missing self but also opened my eyes to see where I am moving in my coming day. This consciousness moved me from being confused, unsure, imbalanced and insecure to being clearer about my meanings. It gave me more clarity on what I am choosing or not choosing to do, and greater security within myself over the security assigned by family, society, position, community, or country.

The journey of having a conscious mind is the selfish act where everyone needs to start their work. This will give you the ground where you stand firmly and walk your path of values, beliefs, purpose, strengths, passion, meanings, and fulfillments. This is the path which you walk with a continuous discovery of yourself, where you get truly connected and reflect the true self. Moreover, at the finishing line you can say, yes this is what I wanted for myself. Again, once you take your next move and start walking a new path, you walk with full ownership, conviction, and authority.

Having a conscious mind is about having a strong secured mind with clarity and certainty. It's when we have no gap between our past, present and future. We have no feeling of insecurity that we need to look to other external sources of people, place or process. We have no feeling of not being or not doing what is expected and we also don't feel like the victim or become worried. A life without the gap between your past, present and future is a life of harmony, being grateful for the life that we already have.

That is what I call the optimal state of having a conscious mind, which is the key to our wellbeing. A person with a conscious mind is someone who rediscovers value, belief and purpose, who reconnects with their deeper positive feelings and who reflects their true and authentic self.

Why?

"Until you make the unconscious conscious, it will control your life and you will call it fate."
- Carl Jung

Oftentimes we get hurt by outcomes of some situations and then we realize that this is not something we like for us. Being conscious is not about limiting those situations to happen again in our life or work. It is not about discontinuing the path to move forward if you don't like it. It is more about keeping those paths open and moving forward, being in the driving seat and having full control over your mind while driving forward.

Having full control means you are able to drive at any difficult situation.

It is like once you are driving a car: you must have full control of your driving seat first, then once you have full control inside, only then can you navigate your rough map.

Similarly, as a leader if you are conscious, you have better control over your leadership behaviours, you are more confident with any situations of change, you are able to be more creative in adversity, and you can take a courageous move once needed.

What?

The first and foremost step of self-leadership is knowing yourself. I am not saying anything different here compared to other leadership writers. But in reality, we tend to work on this last. When we have tried many things, moved a bit further along, we see the success, but we find difficulties in finding the meaning. At that point we have everything, but we also feel a vacuum. If you have ever felt this way, you may restart trying different ways or different things that you may like or love doing. That still is not a solution. You may feel good for a short-term basis. But that does not sustain long term.

This long term and stable good feeling comes through self-discovery.

Conscious Mind

Once we can consciously drive our feeling forward, we can also bring real motion through the right emotion.

Having a conscious mind means making the difference between choosing to walk your success in life or getting a chance of having a successful life. It's the difference between designing your meaning, or whether you go with the flow; whether you bring some certainty, or you remain fully uncertain and unaware of your effort; whether you catch a random bus, or you drive your own vehicle to reach your goal.

Being a conscious leader means:

1. you are navigating your own move
2. you are aware of your core or inner meaning
3. you can recognise the experiences and memories that shaped you
4. you understand the external side of you, the way you behave and act
5. you have a link between your inner strength and outer existence
6. you know for what you stand strong and what you never accept
7. you can find your non-negotiables where you are strongly grounded
8. you know your negotiables where you are flexible without hurting your core values
9. you can negotiate without compromising yourself

In a simple equation, a conscious mind is aware of its thinking and feeling. It can think and feel about a past memory and recognize an older meaning to create a new meaning out of it which makes a difference in coming days.

A Reflection Story

Stuck-state to start-state

> *I took the bus to reach my work. After reaching halfway, the bus stopped to change over the shifts of the bus driver. He turned off all the switches, took all of his papers, ID etc. and put them into his bag. Then he went out and a new driver came in. By the time he was set up all of his stuff to start the bus, a young couple started showing him a map on their phone and asked about the travel time; the bus driver replied cooperatively. Then they shared that they had left their bag on the previous bus where they got off and they wanted to track that bus. With a friendly attitude, the driver suggested how they could contact the bus authority for the missing bag. As I was sitting on the front seat, I silently observed the couple's confused body language. The bus driver asked them if they wanted to go with his bus or not. At that point, they were just looking at each other and not saying anything. They were fully stuck, their logical minds were*

not working, and they didn't even realize that they were holding up the bus and creating a problem for other passengers. Their thinking was frozen and they were not able to move with any decision. Understanding their situation, the driver smiled and said, "I am counting to 5, if you want to come, please grab your seats." So, he started counting, 5, 4, 3, 2....and then they moved away from the front door and took their seats in the bus.

This is just a small situation which made this couple uncomfortable and unsure. But there are many situations where we face discomfort and uncertainty in our life or at work. And the first thing that can happen to us is that we reach the 'stuck state' of mind. Sometimes we become reactive, sometimes we can't accept the facts and we keep arguing and analysing, or sometimes we get ourselves into a cave (a self-zone) where we feel safe to stay for so long that we do not even realize that we are actually not moving in our thinking.

How do you get out of your 'stuck state' and how quick? This is a self-leadership skill that becomes an urgent requirement to remain stable in today's work environment. A few ways out that I may suggest:

1. Break the state by paying attention to something else that will get you out of the emotional loop.

2. Accept your worry or discomfort in that situation, for with any change our body functions differently and that is normal.
3. Think of new solutions from that moment; do not go back to check and recheck with the previous situation, as you cannot dwell there anymore.

Rediscover the new meaning

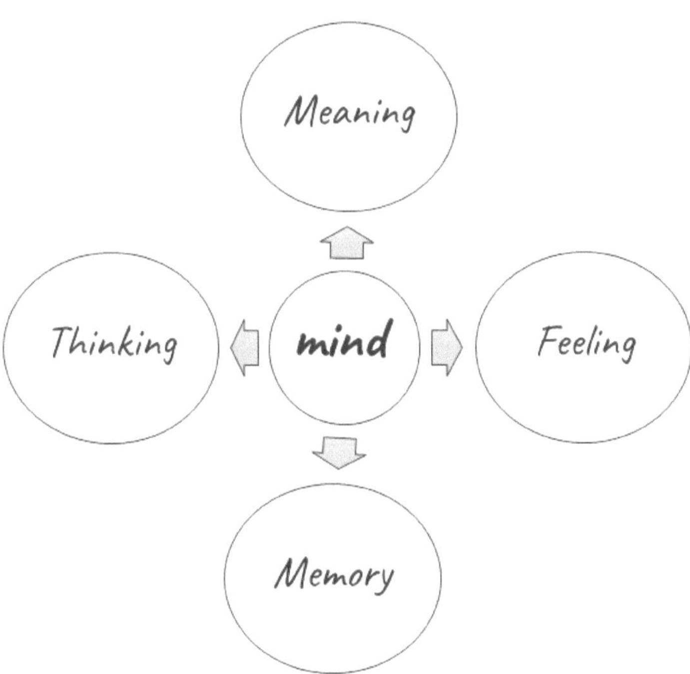

"I INVENT NOTHING, I REDISCOVER."
- AUGUSTE RODIN

Why not discover?

A discovery brings something unexpectedly new, which is uncovered, and not visible before. But here I am talking about rediscovering. At this level of life, once you are already formed and shaped by the combination of memories, experiences and learnings, you can't discover yourself. What you can do is rediscover what you really are and most importantly find out what this means to you now. This meaning is very important as that is the part which makes the real difference between where you were, where you are at and where you want to be.

Why rediscover?

According to the dictionary, the meaning of the word rediscover, in the space of self-leadership, is the process of acquiring insight into one's own character, potentials, motives etc. And the word 'character' means the mental and moral qualities distinctive to an individual, according to the Oxford dictionary. Bringing them together, self-discovering means being aware and conscious about our own mental and moral qualities that we have developed over time.

We all possess a combination of mental and moral qualities. The combination is uniquely moulded over time to create the sculpture, ourselves, where qualities are defined and directed by our surroundings at the basic level of our living. The more we go through some experiences and build awareness, the more we can cross the basic level to the next. And this next level is a closer level to our internal self and away from our external environment, family, society, community and country. This is the level where we can find the answers to the questions that we keep asking of ourselves: who am I?

Why am I living on this earth? How can I bring out my meaning that helps others? What makes me different over time? Rediscovering is a huge work and it takes your tears, blood and sweat to rediscover yourself.

This is the zone of our who, why how and what. I call it the rediscover zone. It's where we are aware of the experience and influence of the mental and moral qualities that are defined by the external environment. And we are also aware of self-directed and self-influenced mental and moral qualities. This rediscover zone allows us to find the interception, the interception that can bring meaningful meaning.

"A highly developed value system is like a compass. It serves as a guide to point you in the right direction when you are lost."
- Idowu Koyenikan

The meaning of self-discovery changes over time. The more time we pass, the more aware we become and that's what we call an improvement. To me, the improvement is nothing but the ability to create a better meaning, especially when you are directing yourself through a change and adversity. You have to let go of the old meaning, you have to start creating the meaning that you want to create, and you have to start owning the new future from now. I totally agree with Matt Church, the founder of Thought Leaders' Business School, who says self-discovery is about going back to past-experience and understanding the new meanings of those experiences that helps you now.

"When I discover who I am, I'll be free."
- Ralph Ellison, Invisible Man

Know your basics to build the rest

Know what you want in your life span of time. Know your non-negotiables. If not, you can't be open to adversity, you won't be able to think creatively, you will not have the courage to move.

Your mind will always be finding a reason of not doing it. You will be afraid to think open and creatively as you are always doubtful of the end result. And you will not have the courage to move on with whatever you have.

Whatever you think or act, you are always hooked with 3 things:

1. Your Memory = good and bad
2. Your Value and Belief = inside
3. Purpose, goal, mission = outside

Value – Individual
Belief – which you generate through life experience
Purpose – The meaning or the why part of your being

To find your values, I would suggest you Google the list of values that Brene Brown included in her book called *Dare to Lead.* This list will help you to find your top 10 values, then make them 5, then 3. Ask yourself why you've chosen these 3 values, and why not 2 or 1? You may see some values are individual or some may be more social - you can separate them. Separating your individual values from social ones will help you to find your core values, because social values change over time once we move to a more socially secured position.

To find your beliefs, always remember that our beliefs are shaped and take new dimension over time. It is important to be aware of your new belief. You can only do so by reflecting on your recent changes or improvements, not by holding on to your past pains.

Regarding purpose, I would say it is an ongoing process. It is not a project, it is an evolution. By asking "what does it mean to me?" you can walk the journey of discovering your own purpose, your meaning of doing everything that you do.

Once you know the meaning,
no rule, restriction, or reason can stop you.

List your values	
Rank them 1 to 5	
Find situations for each and what were your responses to that?	
What beliefs have you grown that don't serve you now?	
What or who developed those beliefs?	
What is your new belief?	

The greatest finding is finding yourself.
The hardest journey is the journey to your inner being.

The strongest power is the power of practising your core values.

Past clue and memory

Looking back and collecting the clues often helps us to get our own back.

Your goals must align with your values, beliefs and purpose, or else you will remain lonely, empty, unfulfilled and unhappy.

How to align your goals with your values?

- List your top 5 values and rank them - now pick top 3 to start working on
- List your top 5 goals and find which goal supports the top 3 value (these are your core or non-negotiables)
- Surround yourself with people who inspire/support you to work on your top 3 goals that reflect your top 3 values

How do you know that you are working without a purpose?

- You work for results only.
- Your acts are implication focused.
- You can't foresee a legacy after your retirement.
- And you end your life without fulfilment.

"A circle is whole only when it reaches to the point where it was rooted."

Add the names of the people who belong to your inner circle:

It needs courage to let go of old belief and to build new belief

"Once we belong thoroughly to ourselves and believe thoroughly in ourselves, true belonging is ours. Belonging to ourselves means being called to stand alone - to brave the wilderness of uncertainty, vulnerability and criticism."
- Brené Brown

I was checking a Performance Evaluation Form which had many behavioural indicators with a range between 1 to 5 for each. It highly triggered my mind once I reached the indicator called 'loyalty and honesty'. I stopped at that point by asking:

What makes someone be half-honest?
Is it really someone with whom we want to work with?

I think we can benefit from the understanding that people are often not honest - with themselves and others - because they are afraid to be authentic and the potential consequences and complications. To be completely honest requires a lot of courage.

How about a metaphor where trust wasn't as brittle as glass but mendable as knitting or stitching or darning or regenerative as new skin over a scar? I suppose the extent of damage determines how bad the break of trust was metaphorically.

Once you are consciously attached to your values, belief and purpose, you are not attached to anything external. You have to detach from the worldly pleasures (facade) of life at some stage in order to be attached to your eternal purpose of life (self-enlightenment).

5. TIME: FOCUSED SELECTION

Staying focused is what we constantly do, by breaking old thinking and feeling to build a new one that is worth investing our mental energy in.

> *"The mind operates optimally when it toggles between focus and unfocused, allowing us to develop resilience, enhance creativity and make better decisions."*
> *-Jinyi Long*

Imagine you are in the driving seat and you need to park your car at the curb side to bring a parcel out of the back door. Sitting in the right driving seat, you aim to park on your left and not scratch or hit the car. To make this simple manoeuvre, where do you need to pay attention? Is it the curb or the car? Only by paying attention to the curb, can you reach the curb. Likewise, in your life, once you are in the driving seat and trying to drive, paying attention to what you do not want or do not want to become is the wrong focus. It leads you to waste years trying hard, but not trying clever.

Stubborn-Flexible

Imagine you are climbing a mountain to reach its peak – you need to be not only stubborn in reaching your goal but also flexible in reaching it.

I am referring to a tough goal when you must be as uncomfortable as climbing the mountain peak.

A goal can be different based on the level of stretch it brings, the additional challenge that you take or by the labelling that other people put on this. Some goals are time-bound, you have not much to do on it, it happens with time. I would say that's not something to call a goal. To me, a goal needs to come with a new level of self-discovery. A goal is something that brings out your true passion. It challenges you with uncertainty, that discomforts you to the highest level and that moves you to an undiscovered level. If you know the 'what's next' in your way of walking out your passion, you are not passionate enough; you are rather limiting it and setting a boundary around by bringing certainty.

A goal is something that brings out your true passion. That challenges you with uncertainty, that discomforts you to the highest level and that moves you to an undiscovered level.

If you are not ready to leave your comfort zone and explore other ways to foster, you are accepting the old position where you are already at. And if you don't move against the winds, you cannot get the ownership of your achievement. It is not something you want for your life, it becomes something that your situation decides for you to have. So, what is your passionate goal that challenges you, discomforts you and breaks your physical and emotional limits? How do you move that forward?

My answer to this is be stubborn-flexible. You must be stubborn in reaching your goal but in a flexible way. You have to be both and in the right mix. Not a bit less or more.

If you are **not-stubborn and not-flexible**, there will be no passion for doing what you are doing. The reasons could be either you are lazy, or you have a time-bound goal where you have nothing challenging to do.

If you are **not-stubborn and flexible**, you are easy to be influenced, easy to be modified, and you are mostly used by other people's agendas. You put a label of 'giving and caring personality' on your forehead to look good, which is actually to gain more acceptance by others.

If you are **stubborn and not-flexible**, you make it unnecessarily hard to reach your goal. You don't see or become open to other ways, you are fixed with the old ways of trying with an old level of emotional or physical involvement which gives the same/similar result that becomes a mental burden that you are carrying for a long time. You work hard but not smart. You are caught up by your ego and status quo. Most dangerously, you don't enjoy or get excited about your goal (which cannot be called a passion).

If you are **Stubborn and Flexible**, you are unsure of how or when to reach there but you enjoy every single moment of the journey towards your passionate goal. You are always certain of your goal no matter if the path is still uncertain and unknown. You don't get lazy in trying different ways. You are open to listening to others and understanding their situations, but you are never influenced or modified by another's agenda. You do not seek acceptance or reassurance by others. You stay excited with challenges, comfortable with discomforts and open to cross old limits with new moves.

Stay stubborn with your goal and be flexible to make it happen. Stay stubborn with your growth and be flexible to work on it. Stay stubborn with your success and be flexible to the drive.

Highly value the time

We often treat time as a secondary factor that depends on how we respect it when we use it. We all have the same amount of time every day, some make multiple results out of it and others stay in the same spot. We often feel like we are running out of time where others are making better use of it. Are they given more time than us? No. It is equal for all. The problem belongs to the way we set priorities for our time.

There might me two reasons behind feeling like you are running out of time:

1. You have overestimated the outcome or
2. You are not using the time on what you need to.

Overestimation is a type of self-sabotage technique that a busy leader likes to do.

Again, using time to do what you don't need to do but you still do them because you feel good, i.e. posting on social media, counting the likes etc. In simple words, you are passing too much time on low value works.

If you are passing your time to look busy or to feel good, you are neither success driven nor ambitious.

Priority is boundary.
Boundary is freedom.
Freedom is priority.

Habit is the fact of focus

"MOTIVATION IS WHAT GETS YOU STARTED.
HABIT IS WHAT KEEPS YOU GOING."
- JIM ROHN

The actual shift happens when you stretch yourself from staying comfortable to do something new. Whenever it is about doing something new, the first thing that our mind recognizes is a threat. No matter if it is just about wearing a wrist watch on your right hand or learning surfing. You have the passion to do something different. You may have a dream to make something bigger. And you are motivated enough by the dream. You talk about that dream to others and enjoy passing time on thinking about it. You plan it but do not take any action.

This is our mind's way of feeling good about the dream by thinking about it and making it comfortable for us. But any action that you take by breaking your regular routine is a source of discomfort. And your mind will treat it like a bungy jump.

I remember my mouth was officially shut for 2 years after moving to Australia. Even after conducting more than half a century of training at top MNC companies, I was so much into a 'stuck state' with my speaking in an English speaking country that I forgot about my 10 years of speaking in English to audiences including students.

"We first make our habits,
and then our habits make us."
- John Dryden

Breaking this pattern was so important for me that I could not think about moving ahead with my career without it. So, I started with small talk with my son. Then I started talking to the marketing people over the phone. I listened to them for hours and responded over the phone. It was safe for me because I didn't see them, and they didn't see me either. Once I started feeling comfortable, I started doing small workshops for migrant women. Meanwhile I continued my learning on my subject matter in depth as well.

So, setting your mind is the most important thing. You have to set your mind without having a drop of doubt in it. You need to dedicate all your thinking and consistency into the focus. Because, whenever you start doing that, the number one thing that will not work along by itself is your mind. Even for patients who have undergone bypass surgery, only one in nine adopts healthier day-to-day habits. Anything that you do must be linked with your focus. You must eat, sleep and shit the focus. And that comes through a huge level of clarity:

- you need to get clarity on where you see yourself
- what do you mean by your full focus
- how do you stay creative with owning your core competency

- how do you identify your biggest self-doubt to prove it wrong

Even for patients who have undergone bypass surgery, only one in nine people adopts healthier day-to-day habits

When you start focusing more frequently, you will be surprised to see your mind finding a list of excuses to stop you doing it. It will be more active in detecting the errors than it is in making it happen, it will keep finding more danger of doing this than seeing the greater value that it can create.

If you really want to move from the place where you are at, if you have that as your priority, the focus on a small action will make that happen. Focus is like a link between the priority and the move. Knowing what you want to do, where you want to go and what you want to achieve is set to begin when you start focusing on it by little actions. By breaking the discomfort, once you keep that focus on, your mind wires a new connection. And that wiring or connection is called habit. Focus is really simple, just *make it a habit.*

"You leave old habits behind by starting out with the thought, 'I release the need for this in my life'."
- Dr. Wayne W. Dyer

- Now, look again at the Whole-mind Goal Setting Framework® in Part 1 and point to the fixed and growth mindset list.
- Relating to your decision, find what is the fixed mindset you have that is creating obstacles to becoming what you want to become.
- What are the habits that can threaten those fixed mindsets? List them.
- Which habit can help you achieve your 80% by doing the 20%?
- Rank the habits and set the priority to focus on that habit.
- Once you choose one habit, also consider the *thinking habit, a new emotional habit,* and a new physical habit related to that.
- Imagine how having the new habit can change everything.

Habit-malfunction for malfocus

Habit is the fact behind focus. And focus makes it happen for you.

In the book called *The Power of Habit: Why We Do What We Do in Life and Business* by Charles Duhigg, it is explained why habits exist and how they can be changed to make the difference.

Despite a year of trying, some people struggle to change having a wrong habit. A right habit is crucial to the success of a person like Olympic swimmer Michael Phelps, or Starbucks CEO Howard Schultz. Imagine if they had a wrong habit that does not serve their success, what that would look like?

And we are unconsciously creating a list of wrong habits and continuing with them while we are also aiming to change. We are paying our attention to the wrong things, which divert our focus from what we want to become to what we do not want to become. And more dangerously, by doing this we are developing a new wiring, new habits of what we do not want to become. This is what I call the habit-malfunction for malfocus.

To shift your focus on a long term change, your attention to problems, short term results and performance will not work. Your attention has to be paid more frequently to solution, impact and effort. In simple terms:

- **How**: Focus the solution, not the problem detail
- **What**: Focus the impact, not the result only
- **Who**: Focus the effort, not the performance only

20: 80 to 80:20

We mostly pay narrow attention and choose a quick solution. What we are afraid to do is aim for a lasting solution with a broad focus.

It's the world of multitasking and it's hardly possible to give someone our undivided attention. We often speak to others while checking emails, checking our phone or thinking about the project we are currently working on. Once you are speaking to someone, you are not only sharing the words, you are also sending and receiving beyond words. But if you are not paying attention you may receive the words, but you miss the rest. This may result in you exchanging 20% and missing the 80%, missing the great opportunity of insights and meaning just because of your narrow attention.

In a busy world, we mostly pay **narrow attention and look for a quick solution**. What we are afraid to do is aim for a **lasting solution with a broad focus**. And because of the narrow focus and quick solution, I have seen people are struggling in their relationships with their boss, partners, family members, peers. They end up spending more time and sometimes money by having a consultant to minimise the gap. The simple act that we can start doing is listening actively. Ask yourself:

When was the last time I made proper eye contact in a conversation?
Start practicing active listening.

Once you are focused, you take over time.
Once you are passionate, you take over the deadline.

Intention to investment

If you have intention to get something that really matters to you, invest, and invest your full focus on that. You need to get your focus right. No matter what happens to your life, no matter what comes in between, no matter how badly you get interrupted, disrupted or interfered, keep your focus on. Be aware of your thinking and navigate toward the right direction.

In difficult situations, it is the hardest thing that you can do to yourself. But if you can do that, it makes a great difference. In hard times, in a changing situation our mind becomes an auto chatter repeating and analysing the bad sides of a problem. It is extremely difficult to manage without having strong consciousness and creativity.

"Nothing is less productive than to make efficient what should not be done at all."
- Peter Drucker

- You need to be conscious about the thoughts that are coming, and you also need to learn how to create an environment of creativity, so that you can think for better solutions. This reminds me of a quote by Peter Drucker where he said, "Nothing is less productive than to make efficient what should not be done at all."
- Passing longer time on a wrong thing is not only taking your focus away but also taking longer time to get back, a two-way loss.
- Connection without attachment is the way to be not emotionally driven to any decision.

Defocus to refocus

Our life does not run in the same rhythm. In today's society of connection, it is not hard to stay focused, it is a courageous act to decide to remain focused. It is very easy to get distracted, even with a very small thing. One thing that I noticed is that every time I travel, it takes 2-3 days before I get back to my natural flow of work, with enough focus. Several thoughts keep coming like, I need to be more resilient, I need to stretch more on this, I must try harder, but these options never work. Rather, it stops me being creative and insightful.

In a society of connection, it is a courage to say 'yes' to focus.

And what I discovered, as soon as I accept it and allow it to slow me down, it becomes so much easier to reach the deep work zone. That's how I realized my jet lag is not only defocusing me, but it is also allowing me to refocus by opening a fresher eye to see with a new perspective.

Our mind is not designed to stay focused all the time. It cannot work better if it is focused all the time. Excessive focus exhausts the focus circuits in our mind. It drains lots of energy and makes you become less logically controlled. That leads you to having less control over your emotions and you lose control of your drive. Once you are out of energy, you get back to the older pattern of thinking and feelings. You make poor decisions and are not that open to connections.

Excessive focus exhausts the focus circuits in our mind.

Moreover it is wise to choose your distractions and make it a downtime. That will generate new energy to be refocused.

- You need to learn how to use the disruption time better, how to use defocus to refocus, how to slow down to stay innovative.
- Accept that you will be disrupted, accept that your focus will be influenced and whenever it is, use the mind for the function that makes it better once you refocus.

Prior to Prioritization

How do you know what is your yes? To me, the answer is very clear, by knowing your no.

Setting priorities is one of the most important things that you can do to save your time, your effort and your energy. It also helps you to find a good version of you who thinks, feels and does what you truly are. Once you are able to identify the priority that matters, and you work on that, it manifests.

If you choose the wrong thing, the wrong person or the wrong work as your priority, you manifest that.

- Prioritizing the wrong thing makes it come back into your life again and leaves you unhappy.
- Prioritizing a wrong person breaks your trust repetitively and you feel undermined and cheated.
- Prioritizing the wrong work makes you overwhelmed, anxious and stressed which reflects in everything in your life.

Setting a wrong priority brings out the bad version of you who thinks, feels and acts against your true self.

If you find that you are doing everything but still feeling unhappy, undermined, undervalued; if you find you cannot trust easily, or you are simply feeling overwhelmed and stressed, but you don't know why, I would say you may need to check your priority. You can only know your priority once you know what it is not. And saying yes to know your no is the first step of setting a priority.

By doing that:

- You can think clearly about what you really do not want
- You can feel the strong negative emotions
- You can do something to stop that

Check your thoughts, feelings, and actions to know your priority. Identify what ignites you, what inspires you and what is your natural flow of behaviour once you are positively ignited and inspired. That is your priority.

Win the win-win zone

It is easy to choose one who is like us.

It is easy to be on a team that has common beliefs.

In the world of diversity and differences, it is a hard job to work with those unlike us, but it is also a requirement for leading big changes.

In change, it is difficult to keep up with similarities and common beliefs. If you want your people to stay even in a change situation, the only option that makes it work is being in a "win-win zone".

Anything offered without 'win-win' is either a 'win-loss' or a 'loss-win'.

Collectively, this may result in a positive outcome but with a gap on another side.

- The gap which is often filled by one-sided adjustments, considerations, understandings, and support may become a visible vacuum in the long-term.
- But the gap filled by one-sided openness, kindness, and generosity remains an unleashed and invisible vacuum.

The win-win zone is not a commercial or contractual or strategic plan with your employees, clients or customers for a long-term commitment. It is more than that. In win-win, the collaboration starts with acceptance and continues with trust - the currency of growth. There are three stages to reach there:

1. Accept the difference, drawbacks and the needs of both sides. Acceptance gives a mental shift of being

in a secured space, not in a fearful space. A fearful person cannot think creatively.

2. Respect other's time, energy and effort toward a common belief. Change costs a huge level of energy and it also requires time to be stable again. Show respect with every little action others take, with the time they spend and with the effort they take to build a ground of belongingness. A person without a feeling of belonging cannot take a courageous decision.
3. Practice the act of respectfulness everywhere with every action, regardless of how little or big, verbal or nonverbal. The congruent practice builds the trust – the win-win zone.

In one line, respect nods acceptances toward trust.

Time is respect

Respect towards time varies. The time given over the counter vs Doctor vs Specialist are not the same. When we respect other people's time, we also value their time better. When we respect our time more, we also have a higher value of time. We do not do multitasking. We become more mindful.

The respect of time has a direct relationship with the return of the time. The higher the value, the higher the price and better the outcome. We are not only ready to ask for a higher rate but also we pay more to get there. We ask more questions as we respect others' time more. On the other hand, a free offer is not often valued. It comes with less respect, so the acceptance is less.

Respecting time immediately impacts the way we treat our time.

Imagine you need to attend a meeting where you are invited to join a discussion with the senior management team. Your presence at different times gives off different impressions. For example:

Being early: if you are early, it shows the highest respect towards the people you are going to meet or the purpose of the meeting.

Being late: if you are in a higher designation or higher role, you may choose to be a little bit late to show off your higher respectful position.

On time: being on time would show mutual respect.

These are some impressions we indirectly give off with our timing. If you are late, be humble to give notice, and be thankful when others give you their time. Being on time is not about looking professional; it is about being respectful of your time as well as others'.

Once we respect time, we also do more valuable things with it. We automatically speed the outcomes.

What happens when we chase time and don't chase the respect for time?

Chasing time only creates dramas which puts time into a hurried state. Avoid it - you'll not feel pressured or stressed. If you distance yourself from drama, you can be the audience and enjoy the performance of others. That way you also can learn where the performance could be better.

Time to Focus, Focus to Time

Staying focused is the sweet spot between your decision and your emotion. There are too many options to make a decision and all are relevant to our emotions, but the focus is the balance point, a point where you know exactly what you want to do and when. To simplify, focus is the effective use of time.

Focus is a time-based way to have Mindspeed. It is about not doing many things and being able to think in many ways. It is a big decision you want to stick with.

Emails are neither equally important nor equally urgent. Your focus is like your most valued and respected time that you want to spend on something worth spending.

How do you stay focused once you do not want to? Read on!

Time taken to clarify, identify, and redirect is never time wasted

Before setting out for a long drive, it is essential to check the route and the weather. It is more important to know which way we are not taking, or when we will choose not to drive. Being conscious about the Nos makes us interruption free, which will also save our time, fuel and energy during the journey.

Listening to others, does not mean you are agreeing with them. Taking some time to clarify and identify what inspires you, or ignites you is like taking time to find your next turn.
Following and joining others also leads you to find what you like or do not like. You get more clarity on what you chose to do. You are able to identify your intention. Thus, you know the point where you will raise the bar, create the boundary as you now become highly certain on what you don't want in life.

Without commitment, it is entertainment

Your commitment makes the best use of the time that you give to some work or to someone. With a commitment, the time is an investment. With commitment you can do something today that creates something greater and better tomorrow.

When you have control of your time, you can choose which channel to tune in to. Watch the channel that you like to, take the remote control of your life in your hand. Do not let others tune your channel and try engaging you. It is not engaging, it is merely entertainment.

Others give their time to you to entertain you to receive the entertainment back. Your short-term involvement may cause you a long-term commitment. Engage only if there is a long-term gain, not a short term and situational entertainment. DO NOT get anyone to entertain you just for situational happiness. Then you may end up only with entertainment in life, which in other words means your life is full of drama.

Passing a mindful nice time alone is far better than passing time as others expect. It is entertainment for them. Know the difference between commitment and entertainment. And choose it right.

In a relationship, going out without commitment is nothing but a mutual entertainment. Accepting others ahead of your own requirements is giving control of your entertainment into other's hands.

In a meeting, having a conversation or an argument on a topic which you don't want to commit is nothing but entertainment. Either you like to talk to that person, or you do not want to work at that time and you are taking a break.

Life costs time

We live the time.

Our project is time with an ending point. Our life is time with an ending point. Time is the fundamental element to measure our life span or a product or a project. Whatever we do or do not do, it is all about time. Giving our time to a task, project or person is the most precious thing that we can offer. And investing our time on something bigger than us makes it timeless.

All we do with a cost of time.

Because, life costs time.

"The only thing you have in your life is time. If you invest that time in yourself to have great experiences that are going to enrich you, then you can't possibly lose."
- Steve Jobs

6. ENERGY: REFINE TO RETAIN

"If you listen to critics for too long,
you will become deaf to success."
- Matshona Dhliwayo

The source of fuel matters for the quality of living. Trying to be super economic when choosing fuel can cause long-term damage to the engine. Working in a toxic place, with toxic people can cause long-term damage to your health, both mental and physical.

Say yes to find no

"A MAN TRAVELS THE WORLD OVER IN SEARCH OF WHAT HE NEEDS AND RETURNS HOME TO FIND IT."
– GEORGE MOORE

Be curious! When we get curious, we step out of our old, fear-based reactive habit patterns.

Why do you do this? Why do you work in your company, why do I write my book, why do you care about your children?

If you want to find your why, STOP doing what you are doing then observe. You will understand the vacuum which is created is the answer.

Mindfulness is considered no longer as a "nice to have", it's a "must have" because it's the way to keep our brain healthy which supports self-control and helps to achieve effective decision-making capabilities. And we can also easily practice it through our religious or spiritual activities.

We live through lots of surprises in life. We start experiencing many negative emotions and become anxious, disturbed, and uncertain. What do you do in those cases?

We look for a quick solution and we go and ask for other's suggestions on handling it. Sometimes we are too focused on getting a quick solution that we give importance to time over the quality of the suggestion. We don't even think who is giving the suggestion, did that person go through a similar situation or not. And we might end up asking someone who has no children for better parenting tips!

In the same way, we tend to end up with a solution without even looking into ourselves. We don't know what we really want out of our life or don't have clarity about our own fulfilment. That is how we end up being highly influenced, disrupted and manipulated by others or the situation we find ourselves in.

How to bring clarity?

Not by watching news that keeps our minds blocked for a long time.

Not communicating with people who influence our thinking negatively.

Not recalling memories that have a bad emotion associated with them.

Rediscover where your high negative connections are and be conscious about not allowing them to come in again. This is why it is always worth starting a move from yourself first.

Meaning of the Meanings

Stay strong with past self = memory & meaning

Free yourself from all memories that hold you back. Free yourself from being horizontal to time.

Horizontal time can capture both good and bad memories and experiences from the past.

On the other hand, you can also travel vertical – to your deep values, beliefs and purpose or your imagination, ideas and daydreams.

Meaningful new meaning

We are all unique with our meaning. This is our biggest strength as well as biggest weakness. This is our strength when we can direct our life toward the meaning which can multiply and manifest more happiness, success and fulfilment for long term. Again, this is our weakness when we only see and seek short-term happiness, success and fulfilment.

Change the position to change the meaning

Again, the 1 degree of temperature change makes water boil. Water boils at a lower temperature as you gain altitude and boils at a higher temperature if you increase atmospheric pressure. So, you have two possibilities, either raise your standard or stay under pressure.

Past Memories	*Present Meaning*

Motion and emotion

Emotion is the greatest source of our motion.

If you know this secret and use it, you can make your motion.

You need to learn to take the lead of the motion forward, not backward.

And this is the key.

The stronger the emotion you have, the higher the speed you can generate.

Leaving my home country and my relatives, friends and all the lovely things that I enjoyed doing was the strongest emotion that I could ever feel. That strong emotion gave me the stronger feeling of wanting to make something out of the situation...something bigger than me...something that will make my beloved people happier than ever...something that will give me the ultimate fulfilment.

After leaving I was still travelling twice to three times a year. I was doing some work back in my home country and feeling the act of self-satisfaction by giving back. But it was also holding me back from doing something bigger. Something bigger than me.

In one of Seth Gordon's articles, he said burn your boat and do the work. While reading the book, my subconscious mind whispered "this is what you are doing now". I locked my money into an investment in a thought leadership business school. I locked myself, I burned my boat. I kept no option other than doing the job that I always dreamed of doing, to be that person that I always aimed to be.

"Stay away from negative people. They have a problem for every solution."
- Albert Einstein

Bad emotions are good

Our negative emotions are nothing but the clues to our deepest values.

We often have a tendency to identify our negative emotions as bad. That's the reason why we prefer to hide that thinking or overlook that habit to prove that we are mentally strong and emotionally sound.

But...

This is dangerous, as we only get a result which is completely opposite to our expectation.

Instead we feel more empty, depressed, anxious or frustrated.

In brain science, we know that the negative emotion is related to our limbic system, more specifically it's the arousal of our amygdala, the tiny part inside of the limbic system. Once our amygdala is aroused, we start losing control over our executive part of our brain which is responsible for logical or rational thinking.
And then we are...in a big mess.

Bottom-line, managing emotion is a must. We also need to be highly conscious about this. We do many things to manage our negative emotions better and most commonly, we make a major mistake by hiding it or suppressing something else.

Which never works! Most importantly, it never lasts!

We need to make our negative emotions a friend rather than calling them a foe. We instead need to bring them closer to us. Accept them and that will only help us to manage them better.

Here are 3 'R hats' to deal with negative emotions positively:

Reflect hat

Re-frame hat

Restart hat

1. Reflect hat:

Wearing a reflective hat, you start slowing yourself down. Get some reflection time and picture the situation that aroused your negative emotion. List the emotions that you felt. You may get help from Google to find the list of emotions (image at end of book).

2. Re-frame hat:

After getting your list done, wear the re-frame hat. Now look at the list and ask what it means to you. What was the core part that was hurt in that situation? How is the core part related to your life? Or any core belief that you strongly possess? Give more time to each emotion that you listed because these are the core values which are conflicting within you. This is how you can also identify a few which you were not aware of much before. Now, write the values beside each emotion with which it is related to.

3. Restart hat:

At this stage, you wear the restart hat. Now look at the values where you listed each negative emotion. Flashback to the same situation or visualize it. And think and ask yourself, how would you respond to the situation now?

In summary, Reflect to list your negative emotions, Reframe to find your core values related to each one and Restart with a new insight on dealing with the emotion. By this process we can help ourselves to deal with our negative situations more effectively.

Moreover, we can even discover our core values to stand on without being confused.

Mental fuel

Mental fuel is the source of the thought that we bring by ourselves or through someone else. It's the dialogue that we use to speak to ourselves, or the topic we choose to read from the newspaper, or the types of movies we watch or the songs we listen to. All of them can either create a good quality fuel or a bad one for us. As a leader, when your mental wellness defines how well you will decide, and think, on which you will be setting your standard of living, how dare you take a risk by consuming negative mental fuel.

Are you climbing the right mountain?

I was reading the *Thursday newsletter* by James Clear and he always finishes his weekly letter with a question. On this particular week the question he asked kicked me right off the mountain side I had been climbing for a decade: are you climbing the right mountain?

It didn't say a road, a tree or a ladder.

It said a mountain.

And imagine the feeling that you have after spending a key time of your life trying harder and harder with such a passion that you don't even notice the red flags.

Taking a pause and asking this question of yourself again and again saves not only your time, but also your energy. It also saves the mental effort of thinking of a better way to keep climbing it for a decade.

Now after reading the question, even after ten years it gives me a feeling of thankfulness that at least it stopped me climbing.

At least it stopped me at some point so that I could choose a new mountain.

What is your new mountain for the next decade?

What is 'the one place' where you want to put your next 10 years of time, mind and energy into?

It is worth asking often while climbing your current mountain.

Then you know what are the deeper reasons for which you had to stop climbing the old one.

You will be able to avoid the trap of the same thoughts and feelings dragging you toward a similar mountain. And that old one is comfortable, as you already know how to climb it.

Do you want to see the wastage of another 10 years of your mental participation and your energy?

Are you ready to let that bullshit go through your life again?

If not, change the mountain.

Are you carrying extra baggage?

It does not make much difference once one chooses a different mountain but it does if you're doing it with extra baggage.

Changing your flight had nothing to do with your hand luggage weight. It is limited.

If you need to take a different flight, you need to get the extra baggage off your shoulder. Leave that to people who are responsible to carry that for you. You do not need to carry them all. This will unnecessarily take away your energy. This may also cause you to take longer time as you are slower with extra baggage.

Is it necessary for you throughout the journey you are taking?

Is it giving or taking away your energy?

Our old beliefs, old passion, old emotions and old feelings are like this extra baggage. Take your time and find them carefully. Know them closely. Then have the courage to leave it with those who are responsible for that.

Your extra clothing, extra pair of shoes, gifts for the friend you are going to meet are not part of the current time of travelling.

Those belong to the time after.

The luggage that you need after should not be carried by you in flight.

You do not need to put effort and energy into them now.

It is simply wastage.

Just after having a bad divorce, it is not your time to invest in finding a new partner before you invest time on taking care of yourself. After being emotionally hurt, it is not the time to get involved in another emotion that raises the same feeling. It will only damage your condition and keep your wound unhealed. It is not creating room for healing.

We often start climbing a mountain with this extra baggage as we think this has to be taken care of by ourselves at that time. But in reality, it does not.

Lighten your baggage first.

Never carry from your past that which will not serve you in the future.

Do not carry for the future.

Carry what you need for the time only.

And carry the most valuables always.

Carry the most valuables always

On a flight, the most valuable thing that you cannot leave in the back in your luggage is your passport.

Or your money or wallet.

Or your communication device.

These will give you access to other countries. They will keep you on track. They will give you mobility.

They are similar to the bottle of water, food, oxygen and the climbing hook for climbing the mountain.

While climbing up, you need to keep your personal values with you always. If you give up your values to make a quicker move, you are taking a risk of big loss which might be a lifetime loss.

Entering immigration without a passport is of no value.

Travelling without some money is dangerous.

Taking a next leap in life or career without carrying your core values is suicide.

Carry your self-esteem. Carry your self-worth. Carry your standard.

These are not replaceable.

We cannot move our journey in a sustainable way without them.

What are your valuables?

Without which you cannot think about your existence?

What took you from your past to today?

What stops you from taking the next leap?

To me, my beautiful son is the most valuable that I always love to carry. I planned my work and lifestyle based on his comfort and safety. I made the decision of moving home to give him better communication and safety. I choose to travel where I can also take him with me. I designed my life around him. Every dream I dream has him in the centre. I did face difficulties to raise him while pursuing my dream, but when I accepted that as my reality and the most important thing in life to consider, I could also start seeing that everything was falling together. This is my life by design that I value most. I love my work that allows me to do that. For others it is so difficult to manage kids with partners and work. To me it is now a flow of taking care of my son and working on my dream.

SUMMARY: Part 2 - *Emotion*

Having a negative emotion comes with a ripple effect. By having some awareness of emotion, we can allow ourselves to get more control over our emotions. What happens once you are emotionally strong? You find a solution and become optimistic. If you are emotionally weak, you're almost always disappointed, worried, nervous, angry, sometimes aggressive and you are just simply unhappy. Understand your strengths and your weaknesses around your emotion, then you can find the causes behind the stressor of your negative emotion.

Conscious Motion - Being conscious is a journey and it takes time. Throughout the journey we experience many situations and we develop our understanding of life. Having a conscious mind is about having a strong secured mind with clarity and certainty. It is making the difference between choosing to walk your success in life or getting a chance of having a successful life. I think we can benefit from the understanding that people are often not honest- with themselves and others- because they are afraid to be authentic and the potential consequences and complications. To be completely honest requires a lot of courage. It is not so black and white.

Focused selection - Staying focused is what we constantly do, by breaking old thinking and feelings to build new ones that are worth investing your mental energy in. I am referring to a tough goal where you must be uncomfortable, just like climbing a mountain. In today's society of connection, it is not hard to focus, it is a courageous act to decide to remain focused.

Refine to Retain - Working in a toxic place, with toxic people can cause long-term damage to your health, both mental and physical. Mindfulness is considered no longer as a "nice to have", it's a "must have" because it's the way to keep our brain healthy which supports self-control and helps to achieve effective decision-making capabilities. Sometimes we are too focused on finding a quick solution that we give importance to time over the quality of the suggestion. The stronger the emotion you have, the higher speed you can generate.

PART 3

HABIT

Drive to the destination

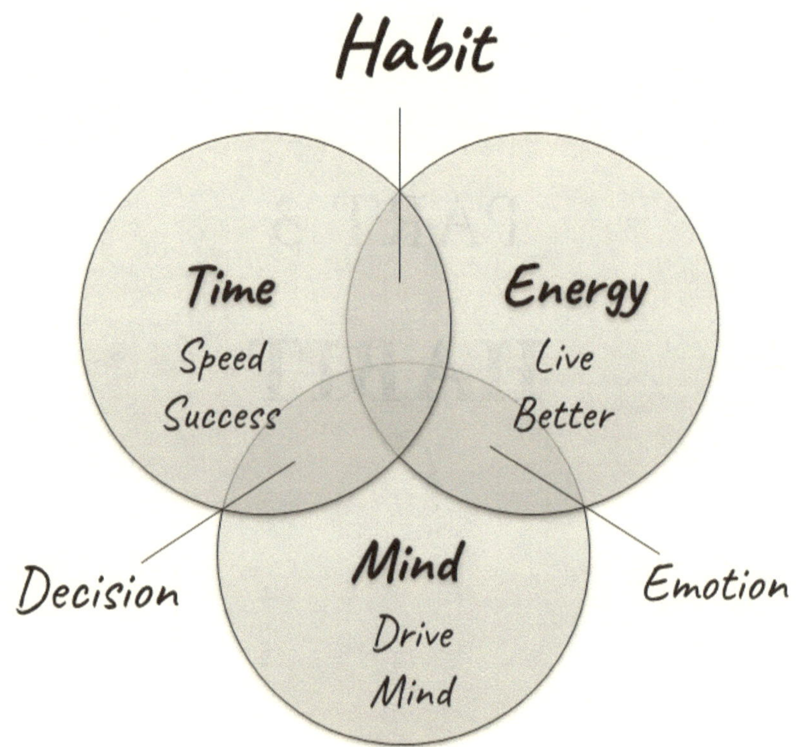
Habit
Time
Speed
Success
Energy
Live
Better
Mind
Drive
Mind
Decision
Emotion

Ambition means change. And change means creating something new that you have not done before. That means creating a new habit. So how does that happen inside of our brain once you create a new habit? And how can you actually do this?

To answer this question, I'll say you can choose your self-directed neuroplasticity. That means you can help your brain to keep up with changes over time, so that you can use self-directed feedback to regain your attention and your positive feedback to allow yourself to change and create new habits. Neuroplasticity and self-directed neuroplasticity are changing your own brain.

You have to understand what decision you took and then you can keep paying your attention toward attending to that. For example, if you say that I want to make a change about my morning routine, so you have to pay attention to the progress you are making on that particular goal. And if you have developed any progress over the time, you have to keep giving the positive feedback to yourself. And that's how you can lead your change over time, and that will also allow you to progressively change your habit.

Mind, Science and Habit

Keep it up

Key Learnings on Neuroplasticity – The Habit Mind

1. ***Neuroplasticity*** *has been the greatest finding in neuroscience in the last 400 years. Neuroplasticity is also known as 'rewiring of the brain'*
2. *Neuroplasticity is the mind's* ***ability to change,*** *which means our brain is not fixed in size and it does change over time.*
3. *'Self-directed neuroplasticity' is your ability to change your brain*
4. *As proposed by Donald Hebb, a Canadian psychologist, "Neurons that fire together, wire together" – meaning that our mind has the capacity to* ***continuously change*** *its functional pattern based on the stimuli inputs.*
5. *According to Hebb's Law, the existing wiring does not deconstruct, and we need to* ***create new wiring*** *through attention and positive feedback to change our mind.*
6. *Emotion triggers old habits. We need to create new emotions for new habits to build quicker.*
7. *Habits are the* ***new thoughts and new activities*** *that create new wiring.*

8. *New habits do not deconstruct the old habits, but by being more mindful, paying more attention, and adding a positive emotion we can develop a new habit quicker.*
9. *At younger ages the brain is more plastic, and plasticity happens from birth until death.*
10. *Bad habits, addiction or* **good habits** *and fascination all affect our brain's plasticity.*
11. *Our key functions for change include* **memory and learning** *which are the result of the brain's plasticity.*
12. *Neuroplasticity can* **help you or hurt you***.*
13. *Neuroplasticity is both Positive and Negative.*
14. *Change of* **lifestyle habits** *are encouraged by changes in the brain - our neuroplasticity.*

7. MIND: CREATIVE ADDICTION

An addiction to take creative actions in the face of adversity is the sign of accepting change and enjoying the advantage out of this.

When you are facing adversity on your journey, when you are unsure about your every turn, you need to be addicted to being creative. You need to be always curious and ready to accept new changes that spark creativity. If you are dealing with a team, you need to encourage them to remain creative by allowing them to think differently.

Think to think

Why do you get paid? When I ask this question to participants in my courses, I often find they answer with things like they are getting paid for their experience, for their leadership capability, for their skill to manage people etc. But when I narrow it down and ask what is the one single thing that you get paid for, whatever the answers were there is one obvious response which I observe – a few seconds silence.

Believe me, this silence speaks a lot. This silence means that they are 'thinking' and yes, it is the only reason why we get paid – thinking!

HOW DO WE THINK?

We may find leaders commonly using the tool of Six Sigma called the "5 whys". This model is simple to peel away the layers of symptoms which can lead to the root cause. It's also good to know the difference between the causes and problems.

If we step ourselves back from a case a little and have a look at the bigger picture, what do we see we are doing here? We are actually dedicating our thinking toward the overall picture, getting more understanding about the problem and knowing the aspects of the present situation. I am not saying there is something wrong with taking in all the details. The wrong thing we are doing here, without even knowing, is that we are not dedicating our thinking enough toward the future, the solution.

And most importantly, the word "why" itself is a negative start to ask anyone anything. Whenever we ask "why", we immediately create a threat-state in the thinking of us/others and that negative mental state stops us from thinking better.

HOW DO WE CAUSE OTHERS TO THINK?

This is one of key tasks of leaders – making others think. As leaders, we often do it while talking/asking/having a conversation with others. This is how we are also leading others to behave. Thinking is the basic way to make anyone behave with their own will power. When we can activate someone's thought, we actually help the person's brain to get the hit of dopamine to act with motivation. As a leader it's also our job not to think on their behalf, rather activating their thinking – and towards the right direction. We need to remember; we are not leading machines, we are leading knowledge workers.

So, how do we do this? I know our answer is – by asking, not telling.

Here I would like to suggest, before asking others, let's ask ourselves: are we aware enough of the thinking that we are generating in others? Is it positive and future focused or negative and problem focused?

Being in leading positions, we need to be mindful that our every single comment, activity and even nonverbal cues are speaking and generating thoughts in others. Everything we are doing cautiously or non-cautiously are the reflections of our thinking. Like many successful leaders, let's also start making a habit of slowing down. This is how we can generate more insights in us and others. And let's think to think.

Let me finish here by referring to a quote by Anthony Jay, the author of the book called *Management and Machiavelli: Discovering a New Science of Management in the Timeless Principles of Statecraft*:

*"THE UNCREATIVE MIND CAN SPOT WRONG ANSWERS,
BUT IT TAKES A VERY CREATIVE MIND
TO SPOT WRONG QUESTIONS."*

Have a dose of daydreaming

EVERYONE DREAMS BUT NOT EQUALLY. THOSE WHO DREAM BY NIGHT IN THE DUSTY RECESSES OF THEIR MIND WAKE IN THE DAY TO FIND THAT IT WAS VANITY. ...BUT THE DREAMERS OF THE DAY ARE POWERFUL INDIVIDUALS FOR THEY MAY ACT THEIR DREAMS WITH OPEN EYES, TO MAKE IT POSSIBLE. THUS I DID!"
- T E LAWRENCE, 'LAWRENCE OF ARABIA'

If you are guilty of passing your daytime by daydreaming, then I would like to join your (positive) guilty team. I spent almost half of my lifetime daydreaming. I often heard people talking to me and asking are you here. And with some blinks of the eyes I said yes, I am listening and thinking about your idea. But I knew that actually in my head I was deep into my experience and thoughts in my daydreaming state.

Daydreaming is not a waste of time anymore. It is not an unsmart investment of your time on thinking about something which is not SMART (Specific, Measurable, Achievable, Relevant and Time-bound). In recent scientific studies it has been proved that daydreaming improves your memory, improves creative thinking and it also lowers blood pressure.

In the field of mental effectiveness, daydreaming is a way of visualizing the end result.

Seeing the result in detail and getting the mental-state ready to be most adaptive to change.

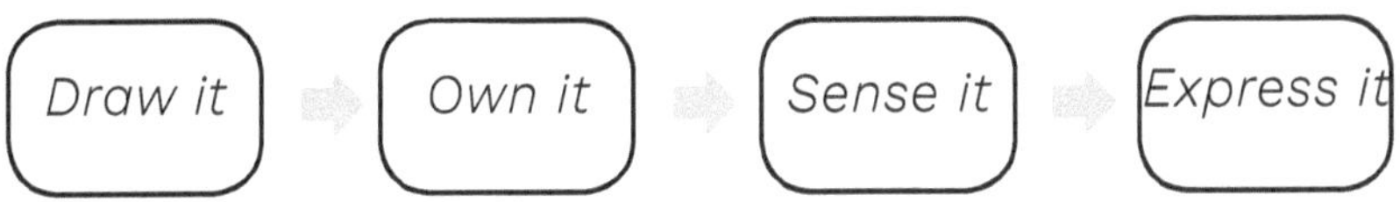

Feeling all kinds of emotions that are related to the change and being able to use the language that expresses it.

In short, have a DOSE of daydreaming to make your way to reach the goal.

Draw it: Draw the picture on paper, colour it, or if you prefer create a vision board by using online tools. Keep it somewhere visible so that you can see that every day and your subconscious mind can have this as an input to keep working on. I love putting it on my phone wallpaper, so every time I turn my phone on, it reminds me of the dream and also stops my random email or social media checking.

Own it: Daydreaming on your career success or about a new relationship is nothing but a process of change. And any change starts effectively when you accept the micro changes related to the big change. Accepting this makes us stay in a reward state and also activates the growth mindset to work toward the change.

Sense it: Feeling is a great way to add passion in whatever you are doing. A right feeling can completely change the way you do the work to reach your daydream. That's the reason why I prefer not to call any emotion negative or positive, it's only emotion; name them, know them and feel them through the journey.

Express it: By expressing the daydream to yourself, you can own it without excuses and by expressing it to others (not to 'energy drainers') you can also get more motivational neurochemicals which will get your whole body ready to act on it.

Research published in *Perspectives on Psychological Science* indicates that looking inward and reflecting through daydreaming can help us better build memories and improve our attention spans.

Moreover, daydreaming is a good way to solve the critical problems through the unconscious mind. It increases the IQ by having a brain rest, increases empathy by reflecting on our emotions, it taps into the working memory and is also good for our well-being.

Do daydream. Take a dose of daydream every day, it will foster your way towards the goal.

IMAGINATION DOES NOT BECOME GREAT UNTIL HUMAN BEINGS, GIVEN THE COURAGE AND THE STRENGTH, USE IT TO CREATE.
- MARIA MONTESSORI

Relocate to re-allocate

A creative mind is not something we can teach you to have, it is a way of being.

The most basic state of being creative is doing something which is not normal, not expected and not easily estimated.

Dealing with a complex situation, taking a complex decision, solving a complex problem all require complex thinking, not linear. This complex thinking capacity gives you the competitive advantage over others, which might be sometimes difficult to get the buy-in as they don't see the value in it.

Having creative thinking also requires a capacity to explain it in a simple way that most people understand. This is because you are not the buyer here, you are not the audience here, you are not the customer here. They are.

Change the position, place, or task

Go and clean the kitchen.

Cut some coloured vegetables or fruits.

Go out and sit on a park bench.

Do something different to take your mind out of the same pattern of thinking. This will give you different reflections with some fresh thoughts.

Dance break

If you are in the same mood for a long time, change the mode, change the music, and try stepping to it. Take a 2-minute dance break.

It will be more fun to do with your team.

Adding movement makes you instantly relaxed and light.

Re-allocate to restate

Having a new idea is not the best thing that you can do.

Being able to explain the new idea in a simple way is the best thing that you can do.

We often push ourselves to generate more and more new ideas. We learn new ways of being creative. We often organise training and workshops to teach being creative in a structured way.

I personally have a problem with this process of learning to be creative.

I often question myself if it is the natural way of reaching our deeper level of creativity.

Do we need to take any initiative at all to be creative?

It has to flow naturally and for that we need to learn what makes you feel that flow. This might be different for different people.

In a busy scheduled week when I needed to finish a good number of tasks before we headed into the Christmas break, I planned to travel to Newcastle. Leaving my early morning writing routine, I got onto the train. I started checking email and writing a few things for a current client in the US. But in the process I felt the rush like I couldn't stop. I was feeling like I couldn't type fast enough to catch up my thoughts. I was feeling like I had no time to count how many words I had written. Whereas usually on other morning routines I had to push myself to reach my daily word count. I often felt like the word count was blocking the flow of my creative thoughts. I realised my natural way of being in my flow state is on a vehicle. I enjoy the movement along with the movement of my mind.

Why does this natural flow work better? A change of location detaches me from all the experiences and current agendas that I am dealing with now. That immediately creates a bigger room inside of my mind for new thoughts.

Observe your natural flow state of mind. Capture those moments and lock some time each day or each week for doing that more and more to be creative. This natural state of being creative is like a feeling of being in a different world and forgetting everything around. That is your ultimate place where you are most creative.

8. TIME: ATTENTIVE ATTENTION

Attention is a system of consistently moving the wheels to drive you towards the desired intention.

Attention is a unit of action that you take repetitively to lead to a desired outcome. With a collective rotation of the wheels, you drive your vehicle forward; similarly, achieving a successful milestone is a multi-year journey. It's a journey where you will experience the turns, ups, downs, and ditches, but you must keep moving. You will find some people joining or leaving you, but you must keep your attention right without being distracted by external influences. This is the game of being consistent and gaining incremental reach through attentive attention.

Attention is the unit

"Courage is the most important of all the virtues, because without courage you can't practice any other virtue consistently. You can practice any virtue erratically, but nothing consistently without courage."
- Maya Angelou

The moment before the move is the sweetest spot between the uncertainty and the courage. It is a feeling of fear as well as a feeling of excitement, a lot of visualization of good things that you dream to have. It may be the dream that you've wanted to have in life for so long or the work that you always wanted to do. This moment drives you backward and forward. The point where you start seeing yourself fully ready to move forward, at that very moment you also stand there and drive backward to all the pain and unwanted situations that you faced before.

- Again you start travelling from memory (good and bad) and expectation, perception and assumption.
- At the same time you start evaluating and comparing the life in your logical mind and you keep analysing the feelings that you have, had and want to have.
- You re-examine the person or the situation.
- You look for some evidence, more reasons, a little bit more of everything that could make you step out from the edge.

- And by doing these things you are staying in a loop of thinking but making a real move.

Move is the stage when you break this old comfortable pattern physically, emotionally and mentally and take the lead to create new patterns that will drive your small actions to drive you forward to be the person you choose to become.

"Move is a deep work inside to show a little action outside and staying attached to self and being unattached to everything outside that's pulling you back."

Attentive to attention

Attention multiplies the use of your time.

If you are dealing with an important project with a hard deadline and often find yourself way behind finishing part of the task on time, you are having a problem with your attention.

Attention can give you the comfort of doing difficult work.

Attention is the presence of your conscious, creative and courageous mind doing something.

Attention problems can be cultural which are overlooked or tolerated by the management team with or without being aware of the effect.

High emotional influences can break your attention for days, months, weeks, sometimes for years.

Focused feedback

> *"Even when you hear the word feedback, you can see a brain light up (in an MRI), and you feel a threat response," Dimlow said. "If you feel threatened, your brain shuts down."*

Giving and asking for feedback matters. If you want to keep continuing doing what you are doing, then giving feedback on results will leave your thinking stuck there. Whereas, giving feedback on effort will encourage, remind you to continue putting in more effort. Do not give feedback on results, rather give feedback on effort. There are three types of feedback practices that will help you keep moving rather stopping you:

- Practice **self-directed** positive feedback for your efforts
- Practice **focus directed** feedback for remaining with your move
- Practice **question directed** feedback that supports your move

Feedback to feed forth

Imagine you are having lunch with your friends and discussing how to deal with your teenager. At that very moment, one of your lovely friends starts giving you a piece of advice on how to be a better parent. And you all realize she is not married and doesn't have a child yet!

We are often too quick to make a comment on a situation. Regardless of whether it is over an informal conversation with friends, a board meeting or in a press interview.

As an expert or knowledgeable person, people ask for your feedback because you are the authority. Being in a hurry or being influenced, you may end up giving feedback that makes you wonder how others react to that. And sometimes you don't really understand what was wrong with it. You may settle the matter by passing the responsibility due to their closed mind, their over expectation, or their limited knowledge or judgments.

It is our human nature to always want to stay away from a threat. This is the organizational principle of our brain and it is equal for any small to big situation. This is good, because that is how our brain wants us to stay safe. But at the same time, the quick approach to staying in a safe position may also create misleading guidance for other's thinking.

Giving hurried comments or feedback may also create a gap between your action and your authority. To my understanding, a few reasons behind this are -

- you want to bring a solution quickly to please everyone
- you are biased by your assumption on how to deal with a situation
- you feel overpowered
- you want to stay safe in your comfort zone
- you want to remain liked and seek positive attention
- you use sharing or withholding information as a symbol of social status

If you look inside, you will find it happens especially when you are overlapped by influences or others' expectations. It's when you are surrounded by the noise and hardly can get the information.

"I'M MORE POMPOUS AND SELF-ASSURED AND DETERMINED THAT IF – YOU KNOW – IF THE TRUTH CAN BE TOLD SO AS TO BE UNDERSTOOD, IT WILL BE BELIEVED."
- MARCUS BRIGSTOCKE

We can give quick feedback on the basis of other people's expectations, but not based on your own domain or on what makes you the authority. This leadership move can be good to deal with a situation instantly, by making everyone happy (!), but you are also opening the window of long-term risk, i.e.

- you are not giving feedback where you are the expert and authority which will not sound reasonable when others hear that from you
- you are disconnecting between your position, skill, and knowledge of the situation
- your words do not sound like they will be followed by an authentic action
- you lose trust from others
- and you give feedback without feeding forth

Be Conscious of yourself, be self-assured with your strength. Carry a positive passion to lead yourself, not a passive one. Accept there are areas of improvement and take ownership of doing that. Reconnect your skill, knowledge, strength, and uniqueness to lead a sustainable move to make change. Give feedback based on your experience and expertise that will be accepted and respected. Build the trust from your own ground, because that will be sustainable.

Lonely, alone, solo

Ambitious leadership is a lonely journey. You are the one who takes the very first step and alone. You are the initiator of the ripple. You are the person who takes the first step of walking the road of discomfort over comfort.

It is lonely to generate an idea, it is more than lonely to create something out of the idea. And it's a solo step to lead change. If I take the same statement in a reverse way, you need to be lonely to generate an idea, you need to enjoy being alone to create something out of the idea. And you also need to play solo to take the step forward.

Though every initiative is taken alone, and changing leadership is a lonely journey but calling it lonely or alone is not something I would totally agree with. These two words have an inner link with a kind of expectation in them. It means you are dividing your performance, giving a part of it to another's plate, who could be your teammate, project partner or your life partner. And by giving that part to others means you also accept a fraction of your performance will fail or will not perform the full, which belongs to others, where you have no control, and you are suppressing others over you.

To break the divided ownership thinking, a right framing is important. It is not about reframing or changing the perspective. It is about having a different perspective.

Choosing the right framing can carry the right state of mind.

Leading change is a solo step. The moment when you bring the word solo into your mind, it also follows with meanings like conscious, creative and courageous. You are playing solo which means you are aware of your wholeness, you are ready to explore and walk for a solution, and you are brave enough to take that full responsibility. Having these in your mind can make a huge difference in your presence and in your vibe. That is the beauty of using right framing over reframing. Not changing the perspective, rather having completely different perspectives. That is how you can immediately change your mood in everything. You can start feeling bigger than you.

You don't ask how I can do that alone, instead you say I want that for me. It is not an option, it becomes a choice.

Choosing the right framing can carry the right state of mind.

There is not a single new initiative that has been taken in a group. It is always sourced from an individual. Over time, when other people find some common benefit, they join, leave or re-join.

You need to be lonely to generate an idea, and you need to enjoy being alone to create something out of it.

Join: because it looks like supporting the same value, belief or purpose

Leave: as it already solved the purpose or is contra to other values

Re-join: re-join when they find the initiative is creating continuous value

Once you are on a mission of change, you are on a solo journey. On your journey, some will join you, some will leave you and some will re-join you.

Those who join you on your journey, they join as they see some spaces where they have some similarity of their own purpose as well. Over time, some people find it not aligned with a part of their purpose and they choose to leave. Sometimes they find an easier way to their purpose and may even forget their values while thinking about the way to reach their goal, or they are not conscious enough about their non-negotiables.

Those who re-join you on your journey see some common space elsewhere to share their own values. But over time they find the other way was not supporting their core values and they leave that path and join you again. It happens because they rediscover their core values. They may get influenced in weak moments but that does not last.

Join – leave = not sure about the core values and takeaways overlapping values

Join – leave – re-join = sure about the core values and take other ways but leave those and re-join where values match.

A bold act builds bigger self-trust

"You cannot be brave without disappointing some people."
- Oprah Winfrey

In a discussion between Oprah Winfrey and Brené Brown about how to live a brave life, Oprah stated this quote. This is so true, and you also need to remember the same when you are taking your new leap. Do not stop doing what you stand for.She also added, "people who are rooting for your rise will not be disappointed. Only people who are disappointed are people who have their agenda."

If they really care about you and your rise, they will be okay. Moreover, they will gradually understand you and will join you

- People who really mean to stay with you will never leave you.
- You do not need to think about how they would feel. Just do what you want to do.
- They will stay, and they will build a stronger bond with you.
- If they don't get you in a short span of time, don't lose self-trust.
- Do not get interrupted by the influences that they may bring. If they really care about you and your rise, they will be okay.
- Moreover, they will gradually understand you and will join you with greater trust in you.

Clapping is not cooperating

In a theatre environment if you have ever performed or seen a performance, you can relate to this. There are two groups of people in our life - one stays in the backstage and keeps engaging and supporting you while you are performing on stage. And another group is the people who enjoy your performance, clap once they like the performance and make comments if there is anything wrong or not.

Being a performer, yes you need to be audience focused but your relationship needs to be more aligned with the people who support you from backstage. The relationship with the audience is short-term and result oriented, but the relationship with the backstage people is long term and value oriented.

In a journey of change, it is vital to face the audience but stay strongly backed by backstage people. In life, our family is our backstage and our work is our audience, whom we need to entertain to get our short-term value. Again, in business, our employees are our backstage people with whom we face our customers to create better value out of our services. It is never wise to pick the work over your family, or to pick the customer over employees or to pick the audience over the backstage.

you need to be audience focused but your relationship needs to be more aligned with the people who support you from backstage

Cumulative collaboration

In a move process it becomes easier when we get in with a group who has a shared goal. With a right tribe, we can share the same pain, we show the same empathy, we transmit similar courage and we gradually grow the trust.

Team and trust

Rita Levi-Montalcini, an Italian Nobel laureate, who was honoured for her work in neurobiology, says "progress depends on our brain. The most important part of our brain, that which is neocortical, must be used to help others and not just to make discoveries." Once we are trusting, our brain is in a rewarding state. We are able see things clearly, we understand the bigger picture, we can take more risks and we are able to think about more solution options. Trust brings an invisible value to the team by creating synergy and by being more creative.

Trust is the single most important thing that can maximize and multiply at the same time

Team without trust

On the other hand, without trust a team is nothing but an illusion of performance. They are together but separated by the direction of their thinking. They are not aligned, and they don't see themselves as a part of a bigger picture. They have their own agenda and they only work on that to be successful.

To distinguish between a group with and without trust, Simon Sinek's comment is correct: "A team is not a group of people who work together. A team is a group of people who trust each other."

Trust is the single most important thing that can maximize and multiply at the same time. It creates meaning that is many times better than before and in a cumulative increasing way. Once there is trust the growth and move happen both in height and depth. With trust, it flies high but has a deep root in the ground. A trusted collective collaboration produces the Revolution-Per-Move (RPM) in the outcome by giving and receiving feedback from eligible people.

Multiply and maximize

Sometimes, it's not enough if you already have the right mindset. It's not enough if you are working hard. It's also not enough if your KPI says you are a performer. It is even not enough to have self-reflection on continuous improvement. None of them really matter if you want to leverage your life with a goal that you have not imagined before.

The one thing that can make your move more meaningful and multiplying is having a mentor, a person who is already the person who you want to become. To have a mentor is getting help by a trusted person

- who opens your secret door of potential
- shows your secret ability that you were never aware of before

- makes you to see the beauty of your next move
- helps you to have the insights in taking the conscious and creative step of courageous moves

Past memories are past feelings
Future imagination is a new feeling
Be present to imagine.

One at a time

Start with one to finish the one.

One big thing you want in life.

One big thing you want to achieve next year.

One big change you want to bring in life.

Once you know the one thing, you can take actions that align to achieve that.

Having one big goal is simple to remember, easy to remain focused and mentally effective, as our mind cannot do multitasking.

4A Move Map-Sheet

The 4A table will help you to track and navigate your move as well as keep you motivated to stay glued to that. Have this table printed in a visible place and logging your progress bring your attention and attitude back and will fix your focus on the achievements. And by award or celebration you will be having the dopamine hit to be ready for the very next move.

Attention	*Attitude*	*Achievements*	*Award*

9. ENERGY: FUEL AND FLOW

"When our brains function well, we have the power to tell stories and the intelligence to discern which stories are to be believed."
- Silvia Damiano

When you drive a long route, it is routine to fuel your vehicle to keep it moving. Likewise, you need to take rest to recharge your mind, to keep up its flow and function better. As a human we need to consider our wellbeing, rest and slow down time to be sustainable with your Mindspeed.

Leadership wellness

Self-leadership without wellbeing can perform harm.

If we want to get good health, we can't get it by having a few vitamin pills.

If we want to grow a nice garden, it's not possible to get it only by watering every day.

Similarly, if you are talking about sustaining leadership quality, it needs some practices. It requires something more than theories or strategies. Something that can bring wellness into it, not only in the environment but also cognitive practices. And that is how we can expect a sustaining and influencing leadership practice in the organization.

This is the space where brain science is leveraging today's organizational leadership practices.

To thrive in this new era of work, new leadership models, competencies and skills are required.

We all agree that today is the era of innovation, creativity, and imagination.

Imagination, creativity, and innovation start from the individual level. This is where actual productivity happens. In today's business, individuals need to be more accountable and proactive to cultivate innovation at work. And then it can create the economic value through a group innovative approach.

Wouldn't it be better for organizations to have more individuals with more ownership of their own work without being dependent on the top?

How would you rate your team in being accountable and proactive?

What else could you do to promote that?

"As we look ahead into the 21st century, leaders will be those who empower others."
- Bill Gates

Fuel up to fire up

Think of your brain as an aircraft. No matter what type of engine of model you are thinking about, the most essential thing to keep it flying is the fuel. And it is not any type of fuel. You need to understand the quality of the fuel as well. You also need to maintain it regularly.

Similarly, you need to decide the type of energy you are fuelling in you. You need to decide to take care of yourself to be a sustainable leader. Your effectiveness of performance directly links with your wellness. And self-leadership without wellbeing can cause harm.

Lack of well being is:

- Lack of mental well being
- Lack of ability to perform
- Lack of good mood
- Lack of cognitive skills
- Lack of memory
- And lack of creative thinking

To improve wellness, you need to be aware of the fuel that you are using. There are two types of fuel:

1. Mental fuel
2. Physical fuel

Mental fuel

We need the ebb and flow to create the balance that sustains us.

Mental fuel is a combination of three ingredients. You need to be mindful, grateful and playful. It is a great way to keep yourself in the reward state all the time.

Mindful

Be present. Be empty and open to the unknown, unseen and inexperienced.

Grateful

Be full with what you have. See the limitation as a scope to grow, see the scarcity as a way to think differently, see your adversity as your new creativity.

Playful

Do smile, act silly. Take things in a light way. Have the lightness even when you are working on an intense project. Release your shoulders and take some deep breaths to feel light. If you like, why not to add some fun music as well!

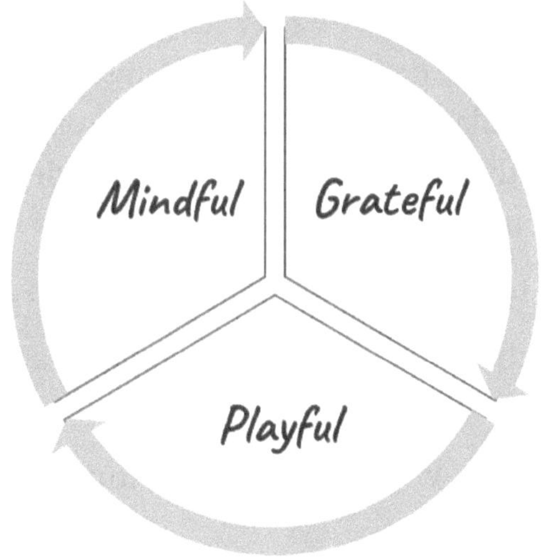

Physical fuel

Physical fuel is sourced from our diet, exercise and sleep. The food or drinks that we consume, the exercise or movement we do and the quality of sleep we have are essential for the quality of physical fuelling. We often choose to consume for the situational pleasure. We do not think about the long term effect of doing it.

"Health is a state of complete physical, mental and social well being and not merely the absence of disease or infirmity." WTO

Eat

Your food can help you to boost your focus and performance. It also can help you to get enough energy that you need to do certain types of work. Like, for knowledge workers it is highly essential to get enough quality glucose for quality cognitive performance, quality thinking, decision making, creative thinking and emotion regulating. With a quality supply of food you can ensure this (check the list of mind friendly food list in the appendix)

- List a few foods from the list that you already like
- Now check with the type and add a few more to keep a balance
- Start with what you like having then move into trying others

Exercise

Physical exercise has a direct association with better mind function. It also saves us from cognitive decline. Doing exercise increases the blood flow to the brain, increases the oxygen intake, and these two are the key ingredients to keep up our healthy mind function. According to science, exercise improves the mood, it can reduce depression and anxiety. Being a leader in the agile workplace, staying out of anxiety and depression is the prerequisite of quality decision making.

- To start with exercise, remind yourself about doing something then doing nothing.
- Give yourself a small treat for meeting your weekly exercise goal. Try to exercise 2.5 to 5 hours each week.
- Doing a little harder exercise, like adding 5 more push ups, or running 5 extra minutes will not only build your physical strength but also will create the mindset of stretching your limit.

Sleep

Sleep takes one third of our lifetime. Sleep is the great way to refuel the energy of our mind. And this refuelling is associated with getting our mind ready for quality thinking including decision making and creative problem solving, analysing, calculating etc.

- Sleep helps our memory centre which is essential for better insights.
- Insights are generated through the connection of our prefrontal cortex and the hippocampus.
- Sleep helps build the connection between our short term and long-term memories.

A 20-minute power nap also improves the memory and creativity. It also helps to regulate emotions better.

Understanding the importance of quality sleep, in August 2019 Virgin Atlantic offered an in-flight partnership with Headspace which will help their pilots, cabin crew and passengers to relax the body and mind by allowing more restful sleep onboard. It is crucial for the professionals who are involved in high focused mental functions. Quality rest will help them remain productive, more focused, mindful and happier.

When you are stuck, remember why you started.
When you are down, chase energy.

Self-review:

- ✓ Food list that you like
- ✓ Food list that you want to include in your diet
- ✓ Exercise that you enjoy doing
- ✓ Exercise timing that you want to follow
- ✓ Sleep pattern that you normally have
- ✓ Sleep pattern that you want to include in your schedule

Accept yourself first

In a talk by Lisa Nichols she said love others from your saucer, not from your cup. It was a great reminder to fill up your own cup first. To be able to drive other's energy, you need to refuel your energy. Energy is contagious.

To fill up your own cup, you need to start from 3 core areas:

1. Self-trust
2. Self-respect
3. Self-love

It is a selfish act to be a better self. The harmony of self-trust, self-respect, and self-love can make you full, whole or 100%. Once you are filled with these three, you are also ready to trust, respect and love others. You become the best version who talks to their best version.

Without it:

- You don't get the courage to do anything new
- You are not committed to reach the goal
- You do not find the dedication to reach the finish line

Self-trust, self-respect and self-love comes through self-acceptance. Self-acceptance is the first step to be ready for the change by putting yourself into the reward state. And it is an important part of any person's emotional wellbeing, as well as their physical health.

Be your best friend

How many of us feel good about ourselves?

Self-esteem is a person's overall sense of self-worth or personal value. It is a good feeling when we are successful in the way we find is important to us. If I can say it in other words, it's like riding a treadmill of constantly needing to feel better than others, so that we can feel good about ourselves.

Now the questions arise:

How can we reach our inner peace without evaluating or judging ourselves?

How can we really get free of anxiety and conflict within ourselves?

To me, the answer is "Self-Compassion".

Self-compassion is a combination of three things –

- Self-Kindness
- Common Humanity and
- Mindfulness

Self-Kindness- Relating to ourselves kindly, blessing ourselves as we are. Using good words and practicing good thoughts about ourselves – not criticizing.

Common Humanity- Finding how I am the same like others. Human means imperfections – and it is true for all – accept it.

Mindfulness- Being in the present moment. Living every second. Observing every small thing to feel large. Yes, sometimes we may believe criticism is self-motivation and if we are not criticizing ourselves and being soft or polite, then we will become lazy. We will have less will to drive our dream.

But through experience, I slowly came to realize that self-criticism is harmful. In fact, it makes the situation worse – it causes feelings of insecurity, we start blaming others, become more stressed and can end with frustration and then depression.

Again, if we just look at nature, we notice a child gets a positive feeling of confidence when the child stays close to mom, because they feel safe. Naturally, we tend to respond to warmth, gentle touch and soft vocalization – and it releases Oxytocin and Opiate hormones in our body which make us feel good.

Self-confidence is not selfishness. The more we are able to keep our heart favourable toward ourselves, the more we are able to give to others. When we are happy, we take more responsibilities and gain a happier life being connected with other interpersonal relationships.

SOUL goal

Add your SOUL to any of your goals. The term SOUL represents – System, Outcome, Unique proposition and Love. Having a logical goal is good to monitor, but you need to know your soul goal to give you drive.

System: I put my work and life in a system. Input = here I check with my time, my energy, my resources and my sanity that I need to invest. And Output = my return on investment, how that can add value to my future, what more I need to do for my personal development and what my lifestyle would look like.

But the most important thing is, the input shall be LESS than the output.

Outcome: I visualise the output. That's how I set my mind to start working on it before I take any action. It's easy to visualise something you have already experienced or have seen. If you are visualising something you didn't experience yet, it is difficult to visualise, because according to neuroscience, the brain has a limited resource for working on context. And I try not to visualise only, I also feel it, smell it, and absorb it, making my brain familiar to it.

Unique proposition: I don't believe in the word called 'different'. I believe in uniqueness, my individuality. With my every single 'ordinary' work or behaviour, I keep trying to add something 'extra'. No matter if it is with my colleagues, friends or family. I try to make my presence significant.

Love: It's always true that you do your best at what you love. I understand it's not always possible. Especially when you are stuck in traffic and running late for your board meeting or your boss is praising your peer for the brilliant idea which actually was from you. My trick for this is I just make it up by myself. I turn every single 'hate' act, word or attitude into 'love'. I reappraise and rename it. That helps my brain to stop taking anything in a negative manner but rather as a positive booster.

SOUL = System + Outcome + Unique proposition + Love

Take some time to sit back, have some down time and think deeply (nice slow music can help your brain to activate) about your transformation forward. Start with small things, add a few small new habits – that will bring the big.

Tune, play, sing

> *"We are slowed down by sound and light waves, a walking bundle of frequencies tuned into the cosmos. We are souls dressed up in sacred biochemical garments and our bodies are the instruments through which our souls play their music."*
> *- Albert Einstein*

Tune: Tune in with your inner voice, your story and your language. Tune to play it smoothly, tune it deep to make the rhythm reflect the true you.

Play: Play the notes that you have written over your lifetime. That gave you the meaning of your life today. That brings a new meaning to your world today.

Sing: Sing with the core beliefs. Sing to each other's ears. The ears value the message. The message also shapes them.

A piece of music doesn't sound nice in noisy places. We get noisy and can't even find the nicest tune. We treat them all the same.

We need a quiet place to tune the instruments before we play them.

In orchestras, we all play different instruments, we play our own tunes but in the same rhythm. The differences start to sound nice when they are played in the same rhythm.

The rhythm represents our engagement, collaboration, inclusion, and culture.

So it does in an organization.

So it does with your team.

So it does in a family.

It is critical to align a rhythm while reforming the organization, building a new team or going through a change.

But one act can make that easier, removing the noises.

- Remove the noises.
- Remove the gap of information.
- Remove the biases, excuses, and reasons.

Because it's not about singing it loud, it's not about playing it nice, it is about the right tuning. Tuning with authenticity wins the differences, wins the challenges.

SUMMARY: Part 3 - *Habit*

Ambition means change. And change means creating something new that you have not done before. Neuroplasticity means you can help your brain to keep up with the changes over the time, so that you can use self-directed feedback to regain your attention and your positive feedback, to allow yourself change and create new habits. In terms of creating the habit, we first say that you have to choose a goal or decision that is a whole-mind goal. Give more feedback and that's how you can tap into your brain where we form our long-term memory. And we also have the emotional side of our brain. We can tap into this part, our basal ganglia where we create the new habit by tapping into our hippocampus, where you create the memory. And by leveraging our emotion, which is our limbic system, we are cutting off our amygdala, our negative feeling about the changes. And that helps a lot to create a new connection inside of your brain and create a new habit toward the new change.

Creative Addiction - You need to be always curious to accept new changes, to be more ready to think creative. In recent scientific studies it is proved that daydreaming improves your memory, improves creative thinking and it also lowers blood pressure. The most basic state of being creative is doing something which is not normal, not expected and not easily estimated. Observe your natural flow state of mind. Capture those moments and lock some time each day or each week for doing that more and more to be creative.

Attentive Attention - Attention is a unit of action that you take repetitively to lead a desired outcome. Attention multiplies the use of your time. Attention can give you the comfort of doing difficult work. Attention is the presence of your conscious, creative and courageous mind of doing something. Be Conscious of yourself, be self-assured with your strength. Carry a positive passion to lead you, not a passive one. Accept there are areas of improvement and take ownership of doing that. It is not about reframing or changing the perspective. It is about having a different perspective. Choosing the right framing can carry the right state of mind.

Fuel and Flow - This is the space where brain science is leveraging today's organizational leadership practices. To thrive in this new era of work, new leadership models, competencies and skills are required. We all agree that today it is the era of innovation, creativity. Similarly, you need to decide the type of energy you are fuelling in you. You need to decide to take care of yourself to be a sustainable leader. To improve wellness, you need to be aware of the fuel that you are using. There are two types of fuel:

Mental fuel - Mental fuel is a combination of three ingredients. You need to be mindful, grateful and playful. It is a great way to keep yourself in the reward state all the time. Physical fuel - Physical fuel is sourced from our diet, exercise and sleep. The food or drinks that we consume, the exercise or movement we do and the quality of sleep we have are essential for the quality physical fuelling.

When you are stuck, remember why you started. When you are down, chase energy

MINDSPEED LEADERS

James D'silva

Vice President in Business Development and Strategic Alliance, Telecommunications Company, US

James is a versatile and results-driven executive leader with exceptional customer focused sales skills and a proven ability to develop strategy, build teams, drive change and grow profitable revenues in complex environments. One of his key strengths is leading and executing a plan in a way that the organization can benefit from. As the VP in a leading telecommunications company based in the USA, he was able to significantly increase the team drive to lead new initiatives into the market with increased frequency and revenue success.

Leading as a non-Mindspeed leader:

According to James's understanding, he did not have enough awareness except some useful recommendations related to being mindful and reflective. In his everyday leadership practices, he made some time to reflect, but he also experienced the switching pattern of his mind which interrupted his deep thinking and strategic decision-making capabilities.

> *"I too often find myself not being present and jumping from one thing to another, relying on gut and instinct to get things done quickly."*

Awareness on mind, time and energy:

> *"I would first categorize my day into two segments: work and non-work. This would ensure that I can compartmentalize and turn them on/off as necessary. For this example, I will focus on work thoughts. I would activate more of the creativity and innovation thought processes - the 'deep' thinking. I could conversely limit the quick reaction and emotional thoughts. Taking these actions would allow for significant improvement in finding solutions, empowering the team, and elevating my organization to success."*

Our mind is a key driver to leadership and performance, or at least it should be. Personally, James feels that his mind is somewhat disconnected from his current leadership and performance, at least at a conscious level. But he believes that the ideal state would undoubtedly include close connection between the power of the mind and leadership, that will also ensure the mental well-being which could support and unlock employee potential.

> *As stated by James, "I would say we leverage time and energy as the primary baseline to measure our performance, outcome and success. But focusing on the mind will allow us to leverage virtually limitless potential, significantly improve achievements and deepen team relationships."*

He continues "the mind should be front and centre to drive excellence across leadership and performance."

Leading as a Mindspeed leader:

"Without a doubt, my brain works best in the morning. I am the most creative and most productive before lunch. I work diligently to align my day to support this known fact. Specifically, I get up and start working very early and typically have 2 to 3 hours of dedicated time before meetings start. I also work to scheduled brainstorming and deep thought meetings before lunch. After lunch, it is typically updates and information sharing meetings which I can consume. I also realize that evenings are not my strength from a cognitive standpoint and thus work to avoid certain types of meetings and discussions. There is always room for improvement, but I have learned myself well enough to know when I work best and how to align my day to support my natural flows and functions. On a side note, this is almost 100% opposite of my CEO, with whom I work with very closely. It does present challenges and requires compromise to ensure we are both at a peak when deep creative thinking is required." - James.

Key insights:

James prefers to attend meetings and get brainstorming done in the morning when his mind is mostly ready for quality thinking. He balances his productivity by moving updates or information sharing related activities after lunch.

His thought process follows a flow like this: work thoughts > creativity and innovation > deep thinking > removing emotional thoughts = finding a solution.

At a team level, he often implements conscious empowerment through cascading tasks in which he delegates the task without telling people what to do. He prefers to encourage them and provide them enough space to think on their own. By applying this method, he facilitates their maximum cognitive capacity. He treats mind as being at the front and centre that brings excellence across leadership and performance.

Source: University of Denver, Head and Heart of Leadership course participants.

Sir Richard Branson

English business magnate, investor, author and philanthropist

"A BUSINESS HAS TO BE INVOLVING, IT HAS TO BE FUN, AND IT HAS TO EXERCISE YOUR CREATIVE INSTINCTS."
– RICHARD BRANSON

Sir Richard Branson is one of the most successful entrepreneurs and the most iconic persona in today's business world. It's incredible that he managed to start up his first business venture at 16, given the fact that he had poor academic performance and dropped out of school at age 13 with dyslexia. Richard launched a magazine called Student in 1966, and today his Virgin companies are renowned worldwide. He is a perfect role model in taking high risk, breaking boundaries and leading changes with purpose.

> *"I wanted to be an editor or a journalist. I wasn't really interested in being an entrepreneur, but I soon found I had to become an entrepreneur in order to keep my magazine going."*

> *"My mother was determined to make us independent. When I was four years old, she stopped the car a few miles from our house and made me find my own way home across the fields. I got hopelessly lost."*

In an article by Adam Sicinski, he states:

"The primary purpose that drives and directs all of Richard Branson's choices, decisions, behavior, and actions is the act of making a difference in this world. Richard Branson's beliefs and values have been shaped and moulded as a result of a lifetime of unique experience. These beliefs have strengthened his resolve and made him into the man we know today.

Richard is who he is, and does what he does because of who he has become as a result of a culmination of experiences, setbacks, and triumphs. These circumstances have shaped his mind in profound ways, enabling him to achieve incredible feats that have progressively built his fortune and empire. To unlock this mindset, one must look no further than the patterns of Richard's behaviors, decisions, language, and actions."

Richard Branson's Habitual Patterns of Behaviour:

- Courageous: Richard is a purpose driven authentic leader. Stepping outside of comfort zones to face unique and extreme challenges that test his discipline, expertise, and resolve is one of the keys behind Richard's success. He is constantly open to change, always carries a solution-focused attitude. His perspectives, views and approach to any situation is to get the job done.

- Creative: Richard takes time to think and daydream, he daydreams about his passions which helps him stimulate his creative mind to think of new ideas, projects etc.
- Conscious: Richard has a work-hard/play-hard mentality, he loves chasing his dreams while remaining grounded in the real world. He is a person who lives life in the moments, being present and deeply connected inside.

Source: Unlocking the entrepreneurial mind of Richard Branson By Adam Sicinski, http://blog.iqmatrix.com/richard-branson

Thomas A. Edison

American inventor and businessman

Thomas Alva Edison has been described as America's greatest inventor. Edison's signature invention is the light bulb. His inventions contributed to mass communication, in particular, telecommunications. These included a stock ticker, a mechanical vote recorder, a battery for an electric car, electrical power, recorded music and motion pictures. He is also known as one of the most productive inventors in American history.

Keywords: Priority, thinking, focused work, one work at a time.

Orison Swett Marden, an American inspirational author, in his book *How They Succeeded: Life Stories of Successful Men and Women Told by Themselves*, mentions the self-described reason for success by Edison himself. These are a few lines from the book:

> *"I do not work hard now. I come to the laboratory about eight o'clock every day and go home to tea at six, and then I study or work on some problem until eleven, which is my hour for bed. For 15 years I have worked on an average of 20 hours a day."*
>
> *"I never did anything worth doing by accident, nor*

did any of my inventions come indirectly through accident, except the phonograph. No, when I have fully decided that a result is worth getting, I go about it, and make trial after trial, until it comes. I have always kept strictly within the lines of commercially useful inventions. I have never had any time to put on electrical wonders, valuable only as novelties to catch the popular fancy."

"I like it. I don't know any other reason. Anything I have begun is always on my mind, and I am not easy while away from it, until it is finished; and then I hate it. Yes, when it is all done and is a success, I can't bear the sight of it. I haven't used a telephone in ten years, and I would go out of my way any day to miss an incandescent light."

"You lay down rather severe rules for one who wishes to succeed in life," I ventured," working 18 hours a day."

"You do something all day long, don't you? Everyone does. If you get up at seven o'clock and go to bed at eleven, you have put in sixteen good hours, and it is certain with most men, that they have been doing something all the time. They have been either walking, or reading, or writing, or thinking. The only trouble is that they do it about a great many things and I do it about one. If they took the time in question and applied it in one direction, to one object, they would succeed.

Success is sure to follow such application. The trouble lies in the fact that people do not have an object—one thing to which they stick, letting all else go. Success is the product of the severest kind of mental and physical application."

What made him known as the most productive inventor?

"BEING BUSY DOES NOT ALWAYS MEAN REAL WORK. THE OBJECT OF ALL WORK IS PRODUCTION OR ACCOMPLISHMENT AND TO EITHER OF THESE ENDS THERE MUST BE FORETHOUGHT, SYSTEM, PLANNING, INTELLIGENCE, AND HONEST PURPOSE, AS WELL AS PERSPIRATION. SEEMING TO DO IS NOT DOING."
- EDISON

Set the focus

Edison once said, "If we did all the things we are capable of, we would literally astound ourselves."

He believes that we all have the capability of doing amazing things and if we don't foresee it, we can't achieve it. According to him, imagination is the first step of creativity. Then we map the way out, and try and try to reach there. We may fail in many ways, but those failures only lead us to find the right way or the right result.

Keeping a written record

In the book *"Cracking Creativity: The Secrets of Creative Genius"* by Michael Michalko, he says: "Edison relentlessly recorded and illustrated every step of his voyage to discovery in his 3500 notebooks that were discovered after his death in 1931. Keeping a written record of his work was a significant key to his genius."

He used to have a 'Things doing and things to be done' notebook where he habitually journaled to keep him highly focused on a goal until it was achieved. This would help him be fully engaged throughout the whole day or even when he was sleeping or just thinking over his afternoon tea.

Key insights:

Observing the words of Thomas A. Edison, there are a few points that definitely support our mind to stay highly productive at work:

> Being a genius is always a fact of quality focus. It has never ever been multitasking.
>
> Thomas knew his best way to keep highly focused and on one work at a time.
>
> He also mentioned that he did 20 hours work a day for 15 years in the beginning of his life, which he

concluded by saying that when he reached 47 years of age it was equivalent to 82 years. At times he worked 60 hours at a go on one work only. After finishing that he chose a long sleep as his brain refueler. And only then did he move onto a new work.

Edison is a leader of imagination. He imagined the value he would be adding or creating at the end of finishing a work and only then would he start working on it. And in this regard, he never got distracted with non-valuable and decorative work that may have brought popularity, not the value that he imagined bringing.

Passion was the reason behind making him go on. He knew the value he was going to produce, and he was very certain on what he had already visualised. It is also worth noticing that doing one thing only at a time until it was done meant he simplified his work.

Source: https://medium.com/the-mission/how-thomas-edison-described-his-most-productive-days-as-an-inventor-47b2a692c7db

One you know how to consciously involve your mind in courage and creativity, you do not worry about the time, only seeking the energy.

MINDSPEED IN ACTION

As most workplace leaders know, change is constant. Change is necessary. Change is inevitable. It is true today...and it was true 2,500 years ago when a prescient Heraclitus avowed, "no man ever steps in the same river twice, for it's not the same river and he's not the same man."

We could say the same about the modern workplace, yet how change is handled varies greatly with vastly different outcomes for organizations. Sadly, mankind fears change as much today as it did in the Greek philosopher's time. Maybe it's the fear of unknown outcomes, of standing out from the crowd, or the fear of making mistakes. Fear can effectively paralyse our mind and our workplaces, leaving us stuck in the mud of mediocrity. Much like any other life limiting condition, the first step is to recognize it.

> Author Steve Olsher spoke of this in *What Is Your WHAT? Discover the One Amazing Thing You Were Born to Do. "Before anything can change in your life, you have to shed light on it,"* he says. *"There has to be a moment when you take a hard look at the truth and contend with the fact it is no longer acceptable. You must be uncomfortable to make a change."*

The purpose of this section is to make every workplace leader uncomfortable enough to then pursue their ambition and lead their organization through change. It builds on the book's coverage of neuroscience and emotional intelligence focusing on the key behaviours – decision, emotion, and habit - and the major resources that we use – mind, time and energy.

Mindspeed leaders

An ambitious leader is a Mindspeed driven leader. Mindspeed driven leaders take a journey of creating new success milestones in a continuous process and our workplaces need more of this type of leader. To keep their leadership continuous and exponentially progressive, the Mindspeed leader must have an addictive formula that gives an edge to make the big decisions, to have a strong hold over emotions and to create incremental habits that also inspire others to change.

Mindspeed vs non-mindspeed leader

Even in a broad conversation, the difference between the dialogues of a Mindspeed driven leader and a non-Mindspeed driven leader are highly noticeable.

Mindspeed	*Absence of Mindspeed*
I know my threat or reward states by being aware of my triggers.	I often find myself reactive rather being proactive to situations.
I have past negative experiences and now I know the new meanings.	I have past negative experiences and I fight against or try to keep me safe from those.
I know my core values and I can stand on this in any situation, at any place.	I know some of my values, but I am not always aware of using them.
I have developed some beliefs, I know where I developed them, and I also know those are not always true. Over time I have developed and shaped new beliefs.	I developed beliefs through my society and life experiences. I strongly hold onto them and develop some new beliefs.
My existence in this world has a purpose. I am aware of my purpose; I consistently work on my purpose. This my feeling of fulfilment.	My existence has a purpose which is directly attached to the people around me. I make everything better around me by fitting in better.
I am comfortable in saying no to anyone who does not practice my values.	I do not say no out loud because it may hurt others and I also do not do what I don't feel right about.

Performance in mind

As a leader, when we say Peak Performance, we do not mean the performance only. We mean more than that, something extra over ordinary.

Organizations state their expected behaviour to us, and we remain very focused on the expected behaviours to prove our high performance. Once we do that, organizations appreciate/recognize us for getting all these behaviours ticked off. We stay happy with the recognised status that means 'you are smart'. And behind the screen, they list us under the criteria called 'xyz player' (assuming the company's name is xyz here). We receive the competitive base, bonus, equity etc. Thus, we happily fit ourselves into a certain comfort zone of performance. Those who are not, are listed under the exit plan or no-growth plan - simple.

Result = I am happy, you are happy and the organization is happy with 'xyz players'.

But, what's next?

As soon as we get recognition as smart, we tend to simply sustain the status. Therefore, we stop trying something new. We have less tendency to take a risk and we do not think 'out of the box'. We stop asking for help from others in a difficult situation. We can become less engaged with others and gradually start finding less connection to the team or organization. Most importantly, we fail to match the right emotion of motivation and our performance falls. We get reluctant and less committed.

Understanding this scenario, organizations plan to develop the performers with a new skill set. They offer a new retreat session to enhance their performance skills as well as motivation. But this investment does not last long, as it can only serve for generating short-term energy to keep performing, not performing beyond. Then comes another plan for the next motivation. And the big picture of the people management system gets stuck here.

Because it's missing the impact of the word 'peak' before 'performance'.

The word 'peak' represents the yet to reach/what else/stretch/undeclared behaviour/freedom/empowerment/innovation. This is something which works as a glue between the employees and the organization. It considers the employee's contribution and capabilities, it connects the missing gap among stakeholders and it combines the individual goal to the organizational goal. It is more about a 360 relationship between the employees and organization - Peak Flow State of the brain.

'Peak' is about having a social meaning of performance.

> *Eisenberger's fellow researcher Matthew Lieberman said, "Most processes operating in the background when your brain is at rest are involved in thinking about other people and yourself."*

Result = empowered employees with more ownership, having more innovation and engagement.

In summary, to get a growing team, we need to be congruent first. We need to have a deeper understanding of the impact, not result. We need to generate a social touch in both top-down and bottom-up approaches. As a leader, it is our responsibility to be agile. It's our responsibility to facilitate the growth mindset among team members, to ask the right question toward the right direction, to understand the emotion of better performance and to identify the true social motivator for our employees.

Having said that, let's check the following areas to understand our present practices:

Are we talking about empowerment but not creating the right environment?

Are we talking about taking a risk, but still having a fixed set of competencies?

Are we investing in our people without tapping into their right emotion?

Are we focusing on the future while having a conversation based on the past?

Take some time to reflect on these questions. You will understand the real impact of the word 'Peak-Performance' through implementing the ideas of Mindspeed.

Change in mind

In the knowledge economy, where people are being paid to think, and with constant change, there is more pressure than ever to improve how we think, behave and perform.

The suggested findings of neuroscience below can help organizations to refocus on the areas of productivity improvement practices throughout the whole organization:

- Practicing mind-friendly cultures that create an environment of creative thinking by reducing the threat and increasing rewards
- Introducing growth mindset practices by progressive communication
- Igniting the passion by tapping into employee's thinking and emotion for lasting performance, which helps the arousal of dopamine, the motivation neurochemical

- Creating a culture of open learning and asking feedback, not giving
- Encouraging the mind-based coaching conversation

This is a total transformation of performance culture and building the ability to bring a positive, lasting performance change in individuals and teams.

A change is a journey of years through right moves, with consistent focus and defined priority. In the process of change to be the persona you want to become, the very first step is to decide, and this is the foundation to accept and step forward. The mindset for doing something different is the key to think, act and behave differently but in an addictive way as you see change as a necessary challenge. That's how you can create the condition in your life that drives the change by:

1. Being readier to adopt the change that you need to embrace,
2. Having more mental control to direct the mental resources into the efforts that matters, and
3. Being automated to invest time, energy, resources, money and mental fuel that facilitate a lasting impact in your life

On the topic of driving change, an open mind allows you to be more creative in the path of adversity and a conscious mind will give you the deep reason to face adversity over time.

Decision, emotion, habit at workplace

The three key impacts of adapting the decision, emotion and habit system:

- Adaptability to change is difficult as it creates initial discomfort
- Behaviour-based approaches impact short-term, not long-term
- People approach connection and persuasion to engage people.

Adaptivity to change

People resist changing even when they want the change. To understand this, let's see the key findings of neuroscience.

Our brain always compares something new to the existing. When we find a new product in the market, we start finding information which matches against the existing one. We keep analysing, then we take the decision. These activities occur on the part of our brain called the working brain, the executive brain – the Prefrontal Cortex. This is the conscious part of our brain. On the other hand, when we work in a known environment, we feel comfortable to make a decision. This known part is the memory part of our brain, which can facilitate us working unconsciously. This part of our brain is called the Basal Ganglia. When we do anything repetitively, we reach our Basal Ganglia which is also known as our habit brain.

How do they relate to organizational change?

If you recall your first-day experience of driving a car to today's performance, you can easily understand it. Similarly, in organizational change people find it very stressful, but once it is done repetitively, they hardwire the new habit.

Again, there is another finding that the human brain always looks at the error or odds first, which is the difference between the expectation and reality. Our brain looks for errors for our survival. The area which is responsible for this is called amygdala, which you'll recall is the part which generates the flight, fight or freeze mode in our behaviour. Daniel Goleman, author of *Emotional Intelligence*, named it "amygdala hijack". This part arouses the stress neurochemical. Once this part is aroused, the brain energy flows away from the rational or conscious part of our brain, the prefrontal cortex.

Change is difficult, it is stressful and uncomfortable. Sometimes, being in a leading role, we tend to underestimate the challenge for a new joiner to an organization.

Shifting behaviour is not long term

Generally, organizations choose the competency based behaviour approach to lead performance and change. The employees are observed and rated on how good or bad they are performing such behaviour. They are rewarded or threatened for the outcome of their behavioural expression. People are given feedback on past mistakes with a positive packaging called "areas of improvements". The total practice drives the attention away from the actual goal. People are pushed to become more conscious of performing the expected behaviour, not the expected outcomes. The result becomes short-term, not long-term and synergy oriented.

Person-centred approach

More advanced organizations make the move with the person-centred approach. They introduce empathy, ask questions, they practice delivering constructive feedback, they also practice being polite while sharing other's mistakes. We need to bear in mind that the human brain is not designed to perform when it receives corrective information or cues. The brain starts behaving like a 2-year-old and automatically pushes back when it is told to do something.

Team without a culture of creativity

After finishing a day-long facilitation with a senior management team, one of the participants was waiting to have a tea conversation with me. As I was done for the day and I had no rush, I agreed. He was a director of a big company and he also owned a travel company. The problem he was facing was with the travel company and he explained the situation was due to his customer service team not having ownership of their work and not working creatively. I was able to help him identify that the team did not give enough time to the customer to find a better deal or package, so if the customer found a better deal with another company, then his company lost them.

In customer service we want quality service and on a timely basis. If the company has a process to deal with each customer, we need to check if that also allows the customer service team to be creative in their thinking or if it is highly defined. Through our conversation, this director was able to see that his team's process was highly defined, in which case he could not expect the team to be creative because that was how their performance was measured.

Mindspeed in the workplace

Mindspeed is a driven formula from neuroscience-based insights in organisational and social behavioural fields. The research findings of neuroscience provide strong insights on organisational applications which support performance, leadership and culture in today's VUCA world. And the beauty is, these can all be easily adapted through forming a new system of decision, emotion and habit. Research of the brain and its functions (neuroscience) has proven that our brain has the capability to keep learning new things, adapting to changes and can keep improving our performance in a relatively short space of time.

Mindspeed based applications, awareness or training can support leaders to connect through conscious awareness, positive emotion, engaging feedback and new habit formation. This approach can boost results considerably over time. It's also a skill set that can help build much stronger relationships with clients as well as stakeholders.

The application of Mindspeed helps the ambitious leader to bring out the passion among their team as well. For doing this, you must -

Be sensitive to how each team member responds to a situation

Recognize that a person's emotional state has huge consequences for their performance. For example, if the goal is to devote five hours a week to generating new business, it's important to consider everyone's emotional responses to delivering on this promise.

> *Dr. Evian Gordon explains that our brain works on two principles: it wants to minimize threat and maximize reward with two modes of operation - non-conscious and conscious. The non-conscious one is quicker and more energy efficient, but at the same time the non-conscious part of our brain gets highly influenced by our emotion and feelings.*

Help people plan their own big actions

You can assist team members in planning when to structure this initiative into their day by using business examples. Concrete action plans have an increased chance of success.

When you plan for the team, the team member's mind doesn't get motivated, encouraged or dedicated to the goal. Rather when they make their own plan, they get the dopamine hit in their mind that arouses their feel-good neuro chemicals and the team member gets motivated toward their own goal.

Ask more questions than you answer

Ask more questions than you answer when someone approaches you for a solution. Use the insights you gain through the questions you ask to lead your client or team member to their own conclusions, rather than telling them what to do.

To get the real insights through the questions, the traditional method GROW is not enough. It only focuses on the top part of the iceberg that has elements of SMART, ignoring the non-conscious part of emotion and feelings. Brain-based conversation bridges the gap.

Pay attention, provide feedback on small progress

Pay attention to, and provide positive feedback on, the small developments made by people to form new personal habits. Have regular coaching conversations. These are separate from your work-in-progress meetings and should focus on the individual team member and what new habits they're forming.

Knowledge based workplaces are not sustainable with a reward-punishment culture. The reward-threat state in the workplace hinders performance, cooperation, creativity, collectiveness, and courage.

Mindspeed based leadership can approach creating a positive work environment which starts from transforming self-leadership changes. On a personal note, from whenever I started learning about neuroscience in leadership, I have been able to see quicker changes in my clients by adopting small positive daily changes. This has also helped them achieve substantial gains in the long term both in personal and professional spaces.

Mindspeed to out-performance

Sam Mead is the HRD in a telecommunications service providing company. While having a meeting on his performance transformation project, he was asked to shoot with 3 challenges he is facing in this area. Without taking much time he came up with 3 questions:

> *How to encourage the team to think differently from the rest?*
>
> *How to empower the team and make them feel empowered?*
>
> *How to make people working in an uncomfortable zone work comfortably?*

The organization I am talking about is an example of a multinational enacting open cultural practice. It has a very well structured practice of compensation and reward system. It was a bit surprising to hear these questions as their key areas of challenges. Yet his organization has a silo mentality among highly competitive teams. Somehow they are still secretly working against one another without being aware of the broader impact.

How could Sam change the way things are done?

How could he make it possible with a big team?

What would lead his people to think differently while staying at pace?

What would lead them to be more adaptive and open to learn or try new options?

In the highly changing environment, people are connected in multiple ways but they are distant in life. Almost all small to big organizations are finding this in common in their teams. There is something missing which is not sticking their people together.

Studies say, even for patients who have undergone bypass surgery, only one in nine people adopt healthier day-to-day habits, even those who are at a greater health risk unless they exercise and lose weight. They clearly see the value of changing their behaviour, still, they don't adapt. And we are talking about changing the behaviour of a whole organization.

This is the space where Mindspeed can work like a glue for driving change. When you can reach an individual's deeper meaning, thoughts and emotions, you also can influence their deeper levels to drive what they are doing.

9 areas, cultural and leadership shift

Leaders as well as the organization can get immense benefits by adapting neuroscience-based insights to lead change, innovation and wellbeing. Mindspeed is the insight-based idea. By implementing the idea, you can promote an agile, resilient and insightful culture which is the prerequisite of change and innovation. And at the individual level, we can benefit from more ambitious leaders.

What are the organizational impacts after implementing the idea of Mindspeed?

9 areas	*Culture*	*Leadership*
Courageous decision	Ownership, vulnerable, Authentic	Agile
Clear intention	Strategic planning, big picture	
Firm fortitude	Mental readiness, acceptance	
Conscious motion	Purposeful, trustful	Resilient
Focused selection	Aligned, paced	
Refine to retain	Mental strength, leveraged	
Creative addiction	Inspired, innovative	Insightful
Attentive Attention	Curious, adaptive	
Fuel and flow	Balanced, wellbeing	

Mindspeed leader as a coach

"Valid questions are better than invalid assumptions."
- Matshona Dhliwayo

To implement Mindspeed at the workplace, the easiest way to start is asking questions. It is the easiest as well as the most powerful way to bring new insights. And a new insight changes the mindset. You can ask the question in a casual coffee break, at a meeting or even at the end of an email. All you need to know is your one decision, the emotion involved and the smallest change you want to bring. That way you will be aware of the language that you are using.

By asking frequent but focused questions, you can help the team's mind to stay at the same pace, you can ignite creativity and direct them in the same direction, creating a secured zone for your team to experiment in new ways. Asking questions helps to build a common ground of trust and it also opens up a learning culture.

> *In Harvard's Business School, the teachers run an exercise in which we instruct pairs of students to have a conversation. Some students are told to ask as few questions as possible, and some are instructed to ask as many as possible. Among the low-low pairs (both students ask a minimum of*

questions), participants generally report that the experience is a bit like children engaging in parallel play: They exchange statements but struggle to initiate an interactive, enjoyable, or productive dialogue. The high-high pairs find that too many questions can also create a stilted dynamic. However, the high-low pairs' experiences are mixed. Sometimes the question asker learns a lot about her partner, the answerer feels heard, and both come away feeling profoundly closer. Other times, one of the participants may feel uncomfortable in his role or unsure about how much to share, and the conversation can feel like an interrogation. (The Surprising Power of Questions, Alison Wood Brooks and Leslie K. John, HBR, May–June 2018 Issue)

"Question everything" Albert Einstein famously said. Personal creativity to organizational innovation occurs through generating information and its meanings. Asking thoughtful questions supports progressive interaction that builds trust and people become more vulnerable to share information or insights. Through asking questions we can tap into others deeper emotions and engage them at a deeper level. This way we can ignite performance beyond. We can create a culture of curiosity and an experimental mindset without fear. It is the most mindful and transformational process of shifting mental capacity to be an ambitious leader.

Ask to think, feel and do

Ask questions that people need to think to answer; ask questions that they can also feel and enjoy answering. And you as a Mindspeed leader, listen; listen how they feel, what inspires them and how they get confused or fearful. Then give them feedback on their progress, appreciate them for what they did well. Show empathy to support them to grow, to sustain. Being a Mindspeed leader, you can foster the progress of success, support to manage emotions and help people to live a fulfilling life.

A few tips on asking questions:

- Ask tough questions first, that will open the conversation
- Use the right tone and apply empathy
- Balance between privacy and transparency

Ask tough questions first

Asking a tough question arouses the emotion of the person. That way you can understand the emotion behind the conversation. Understand the fear of others. Ask the tough question first to create the safe zone, to give an ambiance that you are a place where they can rely on to discuss more to find a better solution.

Use the right tone

Treat the conversation as a win-win ground, show respect to each other's privacy. In a social context, it is highly important to balance transparency because keeping secrets has a cost – mental, emotional and interpersonal.

Keeping secrets has a cost – mental, emotional and interpersonal

> *Research by Columbia's Michael Slepian, Jinseok Chun, and Malia Mason shows that keeping secrets—even outside of social interactions—depletes us cognitively, interferes with our ability to concentrate and remember things, and even harms long-term health and well-being. (The Surprising Power of Questions, Alison Wood Brooks and Leslie K. John, HBR, May–June 2018 Issue)*

Balance between privacy and transparency

To maximize the benefits of questioning, you need to minimize the risks of closeness, privacy and emotion. It is a must to decide on the conversation when other people's feelings are involved and most importantly when they need to take actions based on it.

Think, feel, act to yourself to do so for others.

9 Questions

A question is a powerful tool that we can use to drive Mindspeed with yourself or with your team. Follow the flow of 9 stages. Understand the need to understand from where you may need to start. Below there are two groups of sample questions based on the 9 steps that you may follow to start the conversation. Then you may go deeper where you need to.

Individual level

1. Where do I need to find the most courage to change my life?
2. What do I want? What is my intention?
3. What mental muscles do I need to build to be the persona I am becoming?
4. How deeply do I want this for me, for my loved ones?
5. So, what matters to me and what does not?
6. Who matters to me, how do I create my own social circle?
7. Where do I act with a fixed mindset? How could I be more flexible in my journey?
8. How often am I paying attention to what I want?
9. Am I committed to enjoying the time when I become my dream person?

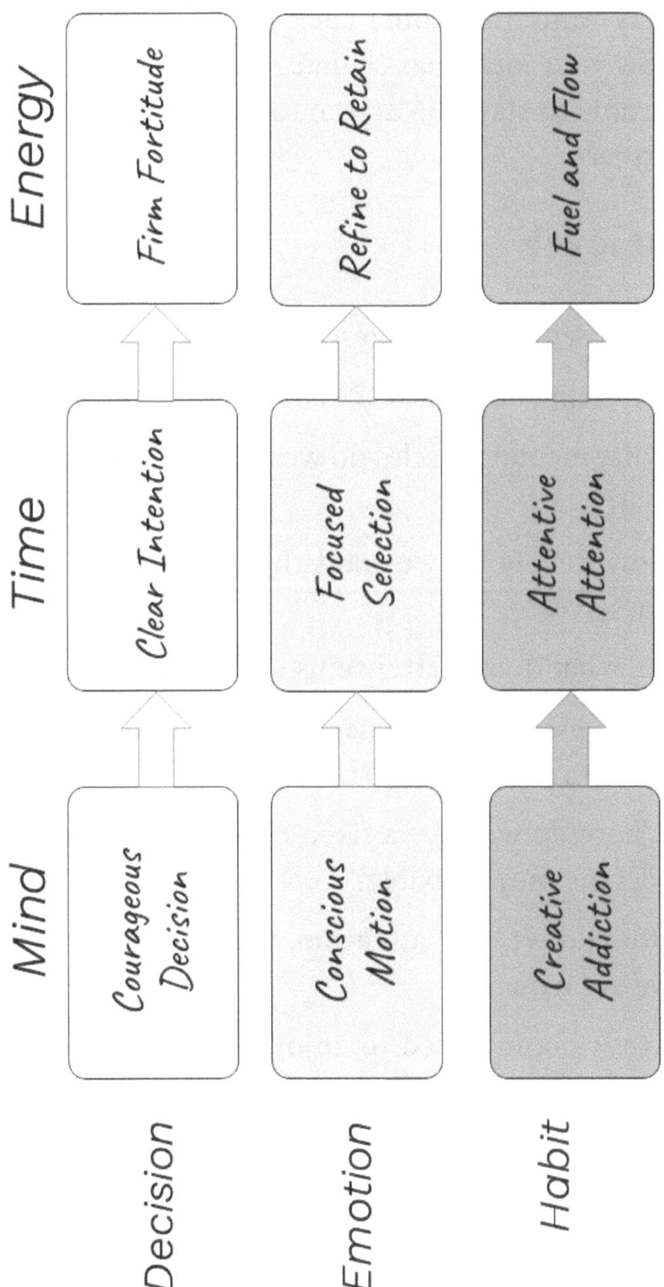
Mind
Time
Energy
Decision
Courageous Decision
Clear Intention
Firm Fortitude
Emotion
Conscious Motion
Focused Selection
Refine to Retain
Habit
Creative Addiction
Attentive Attention
Fuel and Flow

You may randomly come back to these questions and find how your meanings change over time. That way you will be able to stay self-driven to lead your own success masterpiece.

Team level

1. What will be the biggest achievement for the team?
2. What do you all want? What is the team intention?
3. What mental muscles do we need to build to achieve that?
4. How deeply do we want this for us as well as for ourselves?
5. So, what does matter to us and what does not?
6. Who does matter to us, who does not? How do we create a social tribe?
7. Where do we have a fixed mindset? How could we become more flexible?
8. How do we pay attention, what are the languages we are using?
9. Are we committed to enjoying the time when we achieve the goal?

Repeat, Re-appraise, Reward

To help yourself with your progress toward your long-term goal or to help your team to stay at the same pace, asking questions will work as acceleration for their Mindspeed. You need to know how often you need to repeat the acceleration, how often you need to check and re-appraise the move and celebrate the small successes or failures (for trying out something different) by a reward.

A final recap

The Mindspeed formula is a straightforward and clear concept.

Set the decision, add the emotion and create the habit.

It also ensures you attain the the right mindset.

Your right mindset will create acceptance in you to take ownership of your decision. It will make better meanings out of your emotions and will also work behind sticking at your habit. Anytime if you struggle with any elements of the Mindspeed, it means you need to check with your mindset. You need to identify where the fixed mindset is holding you back. Without working on your fixed mindset, you will be exhausted, stressed and overwhelmed. You will take too long, or you will put in too much of your energy.

You can implement the Mindspeed strategy equally for a small or big change, both for your professional or personal scenarios. Broadly, it is an easy three-stage process:

- Set your decision on what to think, how to spend the time and what stamina to build
- Add your emotion by reaching out to your deeper feelings, stay focused on selective actions, and keep filtering social influences
- Create your new habits of addictive ideas, quantify the quality attention and maintain the fuel of your energy flow

To simplify, pick one decision, one emotion and one habit at a time, then drive them through the nine steps.

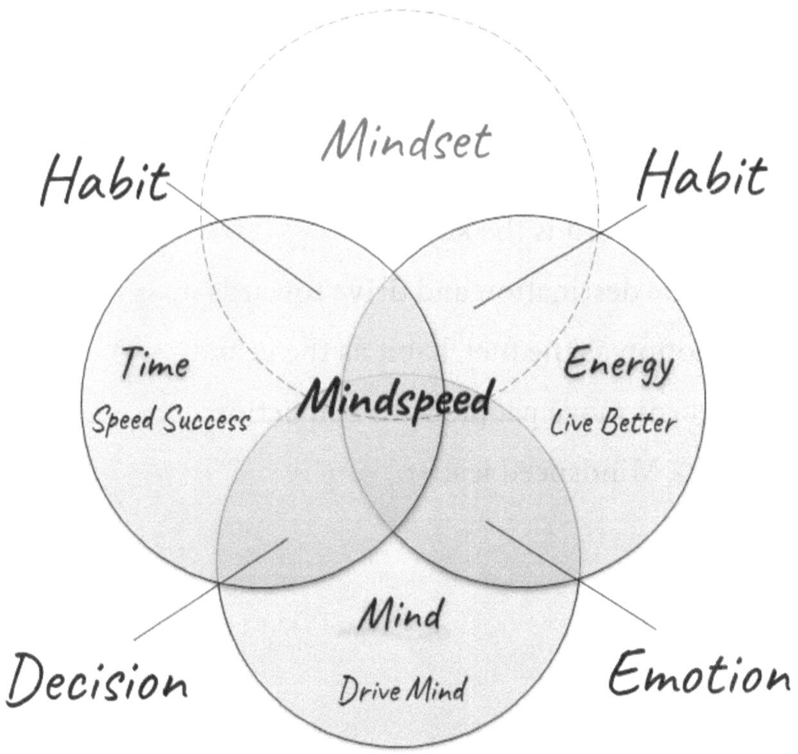
Mindset
Habit
Habit
Time
Speed Success
Mindspeed
Energy
Live Better
Mind
Drive Mind
Decision
Emotion

Work speed ≠ Mindspeed

Human speed is ≠ technological speed.

Human speed is ≠ restructuring speed.

Human speed is ≠ economic speed.

Every human is different with their own speed.

Driving forward is the key.

Decide the destination and drive towards it.

Use emotion as the fuel, habit as the gear.

Your words move people with conviction.

You are a Mindspeed leader.

AFTERWORD

This is my book on Mindspeed.
If you have got this far, you may realise that I give the most value to our mind over our time and energy, because that's where we can get easily pulled over or stuck in driving mode.

In life or work there are many events that may easily trap our mind. The book is a conversation on knowing the science behind how our mind works in decision making, emotion controlling and creating habits.

This book may not make new meanings for some of you, that's ok.

My great hope is that this book acts as a source of insights. I kept the insights part very short and simple without getting into any detail and long stories. My intention is to keep it open for your mind to gain your insights, your meanings and your story out of reading them. I truly believe that having an insight is the most powerful way to accept and apply. And by doing this you can maximise the impact around you which will eventually help you to live better.

I can say this with conviction, because I did not learn about Mindspeed by practicing speed. I learnt it from my shame of having a slow mind.

Onwards

BEYOND READING

If you want to lead a discussion around some of these chapters here is what I suggest:

1. Take 30 seconds of reflection time to write how the idea shapes your thoughts. Then think deep on how this will change your way of life or work.
2. Create a group with common interests or have a conversation with key team members to familiarise them with the ideas. Draw the models and ask more questions to generate insights on how each part of it can leverage your current practices.
3. Set up a Mindspeed Team with 3 to 5 people and play with one idea at a time. Register with Mindspeed online to get the mailable topics. *(https://www.ayeshabibha.com/mindspeed/)*
4. Lead a Mindful Breakfast with your team of 5 to 15. Discuss the model and/or ideas and their relevance to what you and your team are doing. Share your experience and tips.

Stay updated:

The easy way to stay updated with Mindspeed is to register at ayeshabibha.com.

Masterclass:

You may join the masterclass program to facilitate your ambitious milestones. Let us know when you are ready: *https://www.ayeshabibha.com/masterclass/*

Apply the idea:

If you feel the need to work on your success milestones, work one on one with Ayesha and create your path of progress.

Lead the idea:

You can also become a facilitator, get access to the facilitator guide and slide decks by doing the accreditation program.

Experience the idea:

If you like the ideas and want Ayesha to bring them alive at your next company conference, online or live, then email *Ayesha@ayeshabibha.com*

See this idea on stage...

Ayesha understands the hustle of being a strategic thinker and ambitious leader who is obsessed with creating new success milestones.

Her expertise on the matters of the mind as it relates to today's leadership is impressive and the research she shares is compelling. In today's global environment of leading a diversity of teams, Ayesha's wisdom is highly needed. She is able to take a complex topic – neuroscience - and not only make it understandable to non-scientists, but make it entertaining as well. Her presentations are filled with easy to apply actions.

Find out how she can inspire your organisation or your key leadership team to put Mindspeed into action.

ayeshabibha.com

I help ambitious leaders to develop their Cognitive Readiness by using their minds over time and energy. Using insightful language and neuroscience-based strategies, I help leaders to take action for lasting impact on personal and professional growth. In my speaking, mentoring or advising, my number one intention is to direct people's perspectives toward the future, as many are stuck in the past or present—and, thus, confused. If you'd like to work with me to get your Mindspeed moving along, let's get in touch for a plan of action.

Connect with me...

Email: ayesha@ayeshabibha.com

Website: www.ayeshabibha.com

LinkedIn: https://www.linkedin.com/in/ayeshabibha/

Facebook: https://www.facebook.com/ayeshabibha/

Twitter: https://twitter.com/ayeshabibha

Instagram: https://www.instagram.com/ayeshabibha/

BIBLIOGRAPHY

Books

- Brene Brown, Dare to Lead: Brave Work, Tough Conversations. Whole Hearts. (2018) ISBN: 9780399592522
- Brendon Burchard, High Performance Habits: How Extraordinary People Become That Way (2017)
- Matt Church, Amplifiers: The Power of Motivational Leadership to Inspire and Influence, (Wiley 2013)
- Matt Church, Next: Thoughts about tomorrow you can talk about today, (Thought Leaders Publishing 2018)
- James Clear, Atomic Habits: An Easy & Proven Way to Build Good Habits & Break Bad Ones, NY Times Bestseller (2018)
- Carol Dweck, Mindset: The New Psychology of Success, (paperback) 1st Edition. Publisher: Ballantine Books; Illustrated Edition (December 26, 2007)
- Kristen Hansen, Traction: The neuroscience of leadership and performance, 2017
- Cal Newport, Deep Work: Rules for Focused Success in a Distracted World, Grand Central Publishing, 2016, ISSBN: 1455586692
- Steve Olsher, What is Your What? (Wiley 2013). 1st Edition, ISBN-10: 1118644042, ISBN-13: 978-1118644041

Articles

- Ahmad, A. Z., & Tajasom, A. (2012) The neuroscience of decision-making: A review. NeuroLeadership Journal,
- Boyatzis, R. (2011). Neuroscience and leadership: The promise of insights. Ivey Business Journal (August/September).
- Lacoboni, M., & McHaney, R. W. (2009). Applying empathy and mirror neuron concepts to neuroleadership. NeuroLeadership Journal, 2.
- Brown, P., Swart, T., & Meyler, J. (2009). Emotional intelligence and the amygdala: Towards the development of the concept of the limbic leader in executive coaching. NeuroLeadership Journal, 2009(2), 1-11.
- McLennan, K. (2016). Building leaders for the imagination age: A case for the i4 neuroleader model. The About My Brain Institute, edition 1.
- Debbie Hampton; 6 Basic Principles of Neuroplasticity; The Best Brain Possible; August 18, 2019. https://thebestbrainpossible.com/6-basic-principles-of-neuroplasticity/
- Whiting, J., Jones, E., Rock, D., & Bendit, X. (2012). Lead change with the brain in mind. NeuroLeadership Journal 4.
- Paul J. Zak, The Neuroscience of Trust, Harvard Business Review, 2017. https://hbr.org/2017/01/the-neuroscience-of-trust
- Street, C. (2010). Application of neuroscience in executive team coaching: The WSR case. NeuroLeadership Journal
- McDonald, P. (2009). The potential contribution of neuroscience to authentic leadership. NeuroLeadership Journal
- Alison Wood Brooks and Leslie K. John, The Surprising Power of Questions, Harvard Business Review, 2018. https://hbr.org/2018/05/the-surprising-power-of-questions
- Exploring Your Mind, What Makes Some People More Resilient than Others, 2016. https://exploringyourmind.com/makes-people-resilient-others/
- Ayesha Jahan Bibha, Think to Think, 2016. https://bbf.digital/think-to-think

- Oliver Staley, A kinder, gentler Microsoft is replacing feedback with "perspectives", 2018. https://qz.com/work/1380162/a-kinder-gentler-microsoft-is-replacing-feedback-with-perspectives/
- Stephen Shedletzky, Re: How to transform a toxic workplace culture, https://simonsinek.com/discover/re-how-to-transform-toxic-workplace-cultures/
- Businesswire.com News, Virgin Atlantic Launches Sleep by Headspace Content In-flight to Help Passengers and Crew Get Some Rest While Traveling, 2019. https://www.businesswire.com/news/home/20190801005232/en/Virgin-Atlantic-Launches-Sleep-Headspace-Content-In-flight
- Thomas Oppong, How Thomas Edison Described His Most Productive Days as an Inventor, Medium.com, 1017. https://medium.com/the-mission/how-thomas-edison-described-his-most-productive-days-as-an-inventor-47b2a692c7db
- Hokuma Karimova, The Emotion Wheel: What It Is and How to Use It [+PDF], Positivepsychology.com, 2020 https://positivepsychology.com/emotion-wheel/
- Steemit.com, A Day in the Life of Thomas Edison - Habits #3 (Video from 1922 Incl.), 2016. https://steemit.com/story/@cristi/a-day-in-the-life-of-thomas-edison-habits-3-video-from-1922-iancl
- Thomas Oppong, Until You Have Better Work Habits, Productivity Apps Are Useless, Medium.com, 2018. https://medium.com/@alltopstartups/until-you-have-better-work-habits-productivity-apps-are-useless-ff958713d125
- Vo Tuan Son, Win Over an Opponent by Asking for Advice, Medium.com, 2019. https://medium.com/@sonvo2202/win-over-an-opponent-by-asking-for-advice-1aa9cdad2065
- Slaughter, M. (2019, August 21). Reflections on the purpose of a corporation [Blog post]. Retrieved from https://neuroleadership.com/your-brain-at-work/business-roundtable-purpose-of-corporation

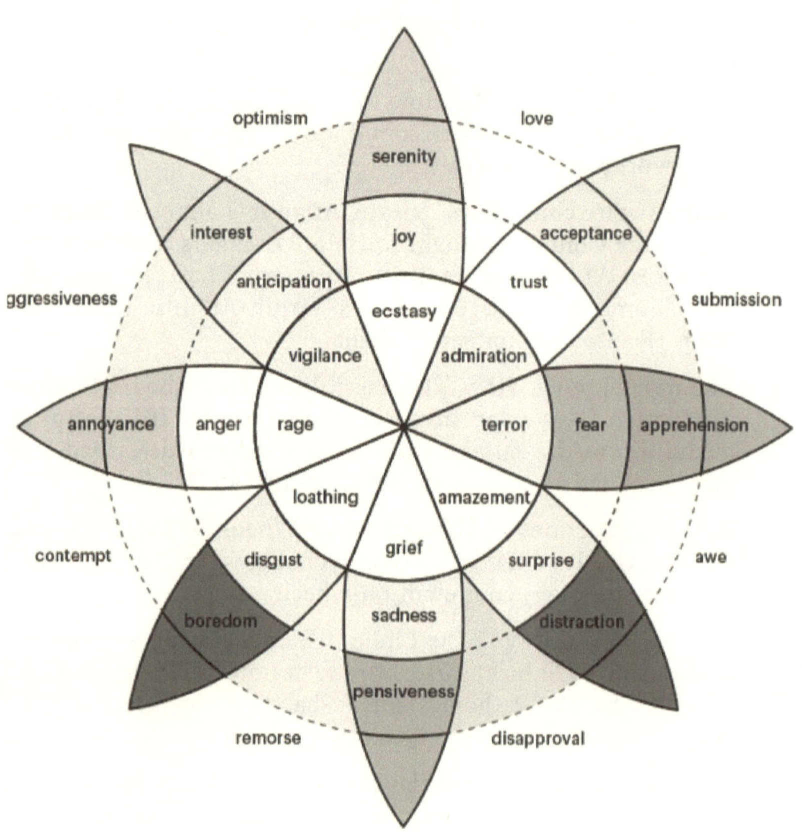

Robert Plutchik's Wheel of Emotions

Made in United States
Troutdale, OR
08/26/2024

22338423R00192